ANDALUSIA

PHILIP'S TRAVEL GUIDES

ANDALUSIA

HUGH SEYMOUR-DAVIES

PHOTOGRAPHY BY CHARLIE WAITE

GEORGE
PHILIP

Acknowledgements

In preparing this book, I have been indebted to Andrew Best, my agent;
Manuel Zarraluqui, Managing Director of Croft, Jerez; Julian de Zulueta,
former Mayor of Ronda; and Tony Venison, gardening editor of *Country
Life*. Also to Richard Seers, Michael Barlow, Dominic Leahy, Alan and
Chris Malcolmson, and Roland and Geraldine Bird. Of the various written
sources consulted, I am particularly grateful to Alfonso Lowe for
his *The South of Spain*.
I am grateful for the assistance of Mundi Color Holidays of 276 Vauxhall
Bridge Road, London SW1V 1BE, who specialize in holidays to Andalusia.

British Library Cataloguing in Publication Data
Seymour-Davies, Hugh
    Andalusia.—(Philip's travel guides)
    1. Spain. Andalusia.—Visitors' guides
    I. Title
    914.680483

ISBN 0—540—01215—7

Text © Hugh Seymour-Davies 1990
Photographs © Charlie Waite 1990
Maps © George Philip 1990

First published by George Philip Limited,
59 Grosvenor Street, London W1X 9DA

Printed in Italy

Contents

To Georgina

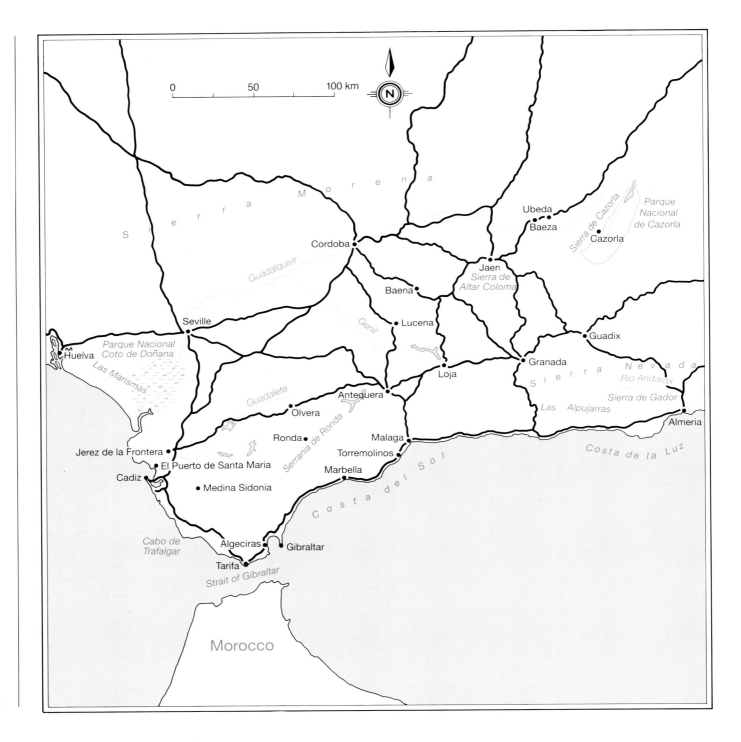

Introduction

The kingdom or province of Andalusia, in local position, climate, fertility, objects of interest, and facility of access, must take precedence over all others in Spain. . . . Nothing can be more striking than the descent from the table elevations into these maritime strips; in a few hours the face of nature is completely changed, and the traveller passes from the climate and vegetation of Europe into that of Africa.

Richard Ford

No-one ought to travel to Spain who is not prepared to bear with Oriental resignation whatever falls to his lot.

Lady Louisa Tenison

Try to get a window-seat, if you are coming to Andalusia by plane to Malaga. South of the Pyrenees the sky will be clear for much of the year, and the terrain clearly visible. Passing Madrid, you will see the great plateau of La Mancha spread out below, patched and striated with patterns of buff or red, chocolate-brown or green, according to the season. Then comes one of the great dark wrinkles that pucker the Iberian peninsula like a rhinoceros hide. This one is the Sierra Morena, the row of mountains which announces that you have crossed into Andalusia, the southernmost province of Spain.

Soon the countryside breaks up. Level ground becomes scant. Traces of greenery are few. Apart from the Guadalquivir and a couple of smaller streams, there is not a drop of water to be seen. Here and there huge plantations of olive-trees fleck the hillsides. Then these too give way to a plunging wilderness. Rocky ridges rear above valleys so narrow that the goat tracks are compelled to run along the crests, since there is no room below. Roads are almost non-existent and the little white villages are widely scattered. At ground level these mountains are barely penetrable, as the Christian crusaders found to their cost in 1482.

Pushing through towards the coast, in the final campaign of the Reconquest, they were trapped in this craggy maze by El Zagal, the Moorish general, and butchered in their thousands.

Two things are apparent from this scene, both of them crucial to an understanding of Andalusia. The first is the poverty of the rural settlements. Apart from the great cornfields that roll down to the Guadalquivir, and the olive plantations, the country has been fragmented by the mountains into individual communities with little arable land. In good times these were vigorous city-states, like those in classical Greece, and many of their encircling ramparts survive to attest their strength and independence. In bad times, which have been the norm in recent centuries, the peasants have been reduced to scratching a hard living from a hostile soil. This endemic poverty – now receding along the coast – casts a long shadow from the point of view of the tourist. The cultural trappings of wealth are fewer than in France or Italy, and more often have a military bias. In Andalusia, castles are more plentiful than cathedrals.

The other factor – this one a benefit for certain visitors – is the region's inaccessibility. The mountains

that have made it poor have also protected it. This is why, only a few kilometres behind one of the most overdeveloped coastlines in the world, there lies a secret landscape unsuspected by most tourists. Inland Andalusia is not merely of a striking grandeur, but also astonishingly backward, often almost untouched by the passage of time. Although the tractor and the car have recently penetrated to many parts, there are still communities where the main instrument of agriculture is the mule, where grapes are still trodden and houses are heated with open braziers of hot ash. Black-clad women, water drawn from the village pump, pagan superstitions and ancient gypsy music . . . all these are reasons why Andalusia has a character of its own, different from the rest of Spain. But the main reason is its history.

The period that left the greatest impact was the Moorish occupation. The Moors conquered almost the whole of Iberia, but their dominion lasted two and a half centuries longer in Andalusia than elsewhere – a total of nearly 800 years. As a result this sector of Spain, stretching between the Portuguese border in the west and the province of Murcia in the south-east corner, is like a separate country, more African than Spanish, the most 'foreign' corner of Western Europe. Set down a visitor anywhere in this territory, within sight of a white town on a hill against an azure sky, and he will find the individuality of the scene quite unmistakable.

The Moorish antecedents are even more apparent inside every major building of any age. Alongside the more familiar architectural styles – and intriguingly commingled with them – are the devices and delights of Middle Eastern architecture: brilliantly glazed tiles, keyhole arches on slender pillars, windows and doors set in elaborate frames, recessed wooden ceilings (*artesonados*) and tie-beams carved and gilded with geometric sunbursts. Intricate plasterwork (*sebka*) covers the walls like petrified lace, in geometric or floral designs, or in Arabic script – but with no

Andalusia's secret hinterland: one of the high valleys east of Ronda.

representations of humans or animals, which were forbidden by the Muslim faith.

Much of this work was not done by the Moors themselves, but by Moorish workmen under Christian rule (*mudéjars*). The sharp-eyed visitor can amuse himself by tracing the evolution over the centuries from an original Moorish style (often military), through the various mudejar blends, and on to the gothic, renaissance and baroque architecture from northern Europe. Some of these later styles have their own Spanish variations. Plateresque work is a form of late renaissance decoration, featuring filigree swags, curlicues and occasional figures: the filigree comparison is inborn, since the name plateresque derives from the Spanish word for silverwork. A later development, the churrigueresque, is a florid late baroque or rococo style named after five architect brothers of the mid seventeenth century.

But the Moorish influence has outlasted these later accretions. It is reflected to this day not merely in the great monuments, but also in much of the humbler domestic architecture. The tiled courtyards that survive in the older sectors of the towns, filled with green plants and song-birds and splashing water, are the desert nomads' recreation of cool oases in a hot and thirsty land.

Their invisible achievements are greater still. The Moors were more civilized than their European contemporaries. Politically generous, except when they were squabbling among themselves, they encouraged the efflorescence of the arts and sciences. Through Andalusia, many of their influences were passed on to the more backward Christian nations of the north. Into Spain they imported a cornucopia of new crops – oranges, lemons, rice, sugar, date-palms, figs, cotton and durum wheat – and a wealth of new skills. Their farmers criss-crossed the fields with irrigation ditches, many of which still survive, and filled the markets of the Mediterranean with their olive oil and raisins. Their scholars instructed the northern universities in mathematics and philosophy, and transmitted the learning of the Greeks. Their merchants traded in minerals, wool, glass, paper, weapons and leather. Their courtiers and architects set new standards of

11

luxurious living, and their capital at Cordoba grew to be the largest city in Europe after Constantinople. As for the silk industry, every village in Andalusia had its looms: the terraced hillsides were dense with mulberry trees, and Almeria, the centre of the trade, became the Manchester of the Mediterranean.

The Moors also, on their arrival in 711, taught the Christians something about fighting. In a single battle on the banks of the Guadalete, 12,000 lightly-armed Berbers routed 100,000 Visigoths. All that was subsequently found of Roderic, the last king of the Goths, was his charger and his golden helmet, and his power vanished almost as immediately. Within two years the Moors had occupied the Iberian peninsula – a task which had taken Rome two centuries.

Then, slowly, the pendulum swung back. For generations the Christian armies ground southwards, until only the kingdom of Granada remained. Two Ferdinands featured in the long campaign. Ferdinand III of Leon and Castile was sanctified for his victories in the early thirteenth century, and is commonly known as St Ferdinand. A quarter of a millennium later, in 1492, Granada finally surrendered to Ferdinand of Aragon and his wife Isabella, the Catholic monarchs, and the Reconquest – the only ultimately successful crusade – was completed at last. In the same year Columbus set sail from Palos de la Frontera, and back to the ports of western Andalusia came the specie-laden galleons that at once made Spain the most powerful nation in Europe.

Subsequently Andalusia faced centuries of slow decline. But its previous history, before the arrival of the Moors, was a dramatically chequered pattern of war and peace, fact and legend, poverty and prosperity ... of the rise and fall of empires, commercial rivalries and international trade. At first, while civilization developed in the Middle East, this far-off territory was only dimly known and barely attainable: early maps showed the Pillars of Hercules – the Strait of Gibraltar – on the extreme rim of the disk of the

Peach blossom amid the badlands south of Granada, near Guadix.

Almost every building in Andalusia, however remote, is regularly whitewashed, sometimes twice a year.

world, washed by the amniotic fluid of the outer ocean. But gradually southern Spain began to play an ever-larger part in the evolution of the Mediterranean.

Where this book uses the word 'Iberian', it refers to the people who lived in Spain before the arrival of traders and settlers from elsewhere. The earliest traces of their habitation are still visible in Stone Age caves at several sites, the earliest of which date from around the twenty-fifth millennium BC, thus predating the more famous caves at Altamira in northern Spain. Later, from about the sixth millennium, there are a number of neolithic remains: and not long thereafter man began digging in the earth to more commercial purpose, especially along the banks of the Guadalquivir, the 'river of the silver roots'.

At this time south-west Spain was dominated by the legendary empire of Tartessus. It was renowned as possessing the richest and most skilfully worked mines

13

of silver, gold and copper in the ancient world. Its capital was Tarsis (possibly Seville), the Tarshish of the Bible, in whose markets all the western world traded. This empire was of long duration, but was gradually eclipsed by a series of invaders. First were the Phoenicians from the eastern Mediterranean, who founded Cadiz in 1100 BC. Then came the Greeks, from 630 BC, and simultaneously the Carthaginians from North Africa: then the Romans, the Vandals, and finally the Visigoths, the last before the arrival of the Moors.

The Greeks bequeathed the olive, the muscat vine – still grown to make raisins and Malaga wine – and a host of legends. Homer set his Underworld here, perhaps inspired by tales of the subterranean wealth of the Tartessians. Hercules too was associated with these parts. His tenth labour was the theft of the cattle of Geryon, king of Erythia, now the peninsula of Isla Leon south of Cadiz; and the hero's name is ascribed not merely to the Strait of Gibraltar but to a number of other sites along the coast.

The Romans were the first invaders to dominate not merely the shoreline of Andalusia but also the hinterland. They imported centralized government, a road system (only recently bettered), the Christian religion, and fighting bulls. The bigger of the *haciendas* that stud the more fertile areas are built to a Roman plan, as are the cemeteries and some of the towns. In exchange, Spain gave Rome some of her toughest legions, plus three emperors (Hadrian, Trajan and Theodosius), a philosopher (Seneca), a historian (Lucan), a rhetorician (Quintilian), and an epigrammatist (Martial). The first two settlements of the empire that conferred Roman citizenship were in Spain. Several traces of Roman architecture still survive, but the Vandals who followed them bequeathed nothing except, ironically, their name. As for the Visigoths, only tantalizing glimpses of their craftsmanship remain.

So much for history: now for a few words about this book. First, a couple of warnings, starting with the food. There are interesting local dishes in many parts of Andalusia, but the inescapable fact is that the Spanish have no tradition of *haute cuisine*. This is offset to a degree by the vigour of the indigenous seasonings – olives, pimentos, almonds and saffron – and by the

Andalusian olives are still picked by hand, by families wielding long poles to beat the fruit from the trees.

fact that the quality of the raw materials is excellent . . . succulent meat, chicken that actually tastes of chicken, and strawberries that bring tears of delighted nostalgia to the eyes. Game is increasingly prevalent, both hunted and farmed: and the mountain-cured *serrano* ham, a more robust version of *prosciutto*, is famous.

It is the bars which offer the most characteristic Spanish food – the *tapas*, or tit-bits, which are always available on the counter. These take many forms: anchovies in garlic, squid, chunks of pork or ham, meat-balls, kebabs, cheese or country sausage, all served with crusty bread. But in a restaurant, the food to choose is the fish. The humblest of the little thatched *merenderos* on the beaches will offer a wide range of sardines and other small fry, squid and cuttlefish, prawns and clams, miniature soles and swordfish steaks as thick as a Châteaubriand. A *paella* is not just a feast but an adventure – a treasure-hunt for nuggets of sea-food beneath the golden rice. Everything is fresh-caught, fresh-cooked, sublime, the best fried fish in the world.

Just as the food varies in quality, so does the wine. Fine Riojas from northern Spain are available on every wine list, and the supermarkets are full of thinnish reds and whites from La Mancha, north of the Sierra Morena, and of commercial blends at astoundingly low prices. But of the local wines the only one with any international reputation is sherry. Montilla, made near Cordoba, is somewhat similar, and some of the northerly regions of Andalusia make their own reds and whites. Malaga makes a heavy port-like red and some muscatel. And in the villages behind the southern coast they make wines that you are unlikely to taste unless you are very adventurous or very lost. These murky fermentations never reach a wine-list. Many never leave their great oak barrels, under the little whitewashed houses, though you can try asking for them in the village bar, if there is one. They are straw-coloured, often with a twang of the muscat grape, and lethally strong. They are not to everyone's taste.

Next, hotels. The problem is that Andalusia is sharply divided into two categories of territory – tourist areas and non-tourist areas. Much of this book deals with the latter. Here, creature comforts are scant, and reliable hotels are widely scattered. And due to their scarcity they are likely to be full. The traveller in the Andalusian interior is like a desert nomad searching for an oasis in which to pass the night.

This means that the itineraries suggested in the following chapters should be undertaken with some care. Check the availability and quality of accommodation in advance, and allow plenty of time for the driving. Spanish road surfaces have been wonderfully improved of late (it is the signposting which is still idiosyncratic, especially in towns), and even small villages can usually be reached without difficulty: but due to the terrain progress can be slow, and there are still a few rough stretches. By far the best watering-holes along the way are the paradors, with examples in most areas. This state-run chain of luxury hotels, often situated in converted castles, monasteries, or palaces, is one of Spain's unique gifts to the tourist.

One further aspect of planning should be borne in mind: the season for your visit. May is the best time. The roadside verges and uncultivated meadows are rich with wild-flowers, and the sun is hot without being overpowering. Autumn is another option – the air retains the warmth of summer long after it has ebbed away in northern Europe – and even winter is never cold except on occasional days or at high altitudes. But do not, if you can possibly avoid it, undertake a driving holiday here in mid summer. Touring Andalusia in August is like crossing the Sahara.

And now two final notes, the first about vocabulary. I have tried to avoid Spanish and Arabic architectural terms, apart from *artesonado* and *sebka*, but you will find occasional references to caliphal artefacts: these date from the period of Cordoba's heyday, roughly AD 750–1000. A *mihrab* is the recess in a mosque which indicates the direction of Mecca, a central factor in the Muslim religion: and the mosque's orangery served as an outdoor anteroom, used for ritual cleansing before entering the main building. As for military vocabulary, a castle may be locally called an *alcázar* or an *alcazaba*.

The last comment is about the routes covered in this guide. Within each town I have not attempted to describe every monument of note, but have concentrated on those which give most pleasure to me, and especially on those which can be covered in a fairly short walking circuit. Be prepared to find a fair percentage of them closed, either for restoration, or, in the case of the churches, because they only open for Mass or are *in clausura*, i.e. belong to a closed order of monks or nuns, or because the custodian of the key has gone shopping. Similarly, my coverage of the country-side reflects personal preferences – for spectacular scenery, ruined castles, remote communities, and for the pervading whiff of history. I have almost ignored the Costa del Sol, and have devoted little space elsewhere to seaside resorts. In between the visits to the major sites, I have herded the reader ruthlessly into the wilderness.

Here, in rural Andalusia, where huge raptors wheel overhead and multi-coloured African migrants flash

into your binocular lenses, is one of the most spectacular landscapes in Europe. It varies wonderfully, almost bewilderingly ... from jagged mountains to rolling plains, from red earth to white, from vines to olives to cork oaks and malevolent scrub. It also varies from season to season. In spring the cornfields are green, and on the hillsides the almond trees are in fresh leaf: but by late summer only the olive plantations retain

Above **The *mihrab* in the mosque in Cordoba. For its construction, the Emperor Nicephoros Phocas of Constantinople sent craftsmen and 16 tonnes of materials.**

their colour, and all else is bleached bare. The little settlements are like Greek island villages transposed to

mountain-tops, washed by a huge sea of exhausted earth and jagged rocks.

There is something else, something to do with the people: the way they are and the way they live. In addition to their unfailing courtesy, they exhibit a rhythm and style of life which is hard to find elsewhere. It is, you gradually realize, the rhythm of the past. The truth is that Andalusia offers a kind of

Symbols of the south: earthenware roofs and quicklimed walls.

escapism which is increasingly rare in Europe: the sense not only that you are far from home, but that you have escaped from the present day.

17

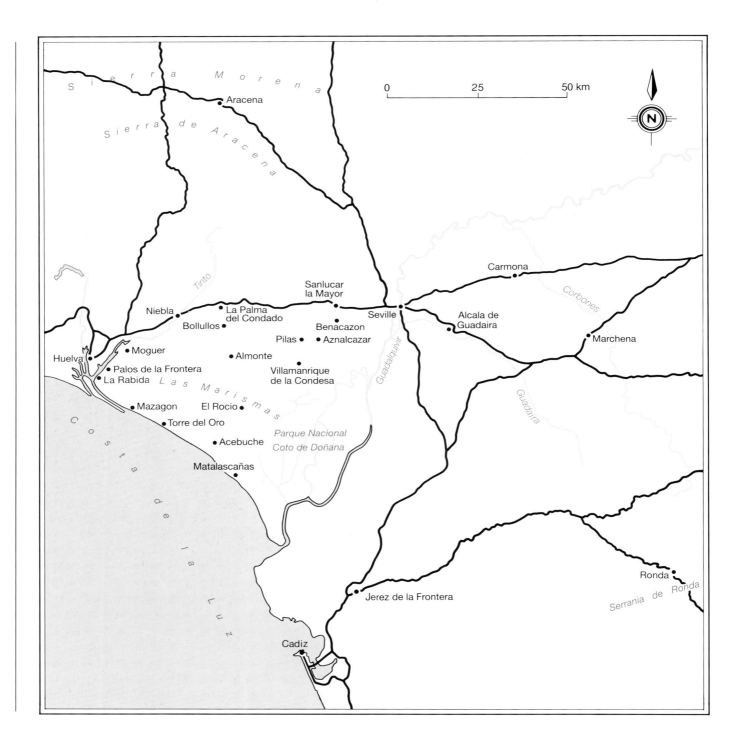

1
Seville and the Far West

Seville – Aracena – Italica – Sanlucar la Mayor – El Rocio –
Coto Doñana National Park and the coast –
Palos de la Frontera – Moguer – Niebla – Carmona

On church and square and market
The noonday silence falls;
You'll hear the drowsy mutter
Of the fountain in our halls.

Asleep amid the yuccas
The city takes her ease –
Till twilight brings the land-wind
To our clicking jalousies.

Kipling

Poor Seville. It would take a far greater and more vibrant city to sustain such a weight of history and such a froth of legend. Founded by Hercules, refortified by Julius Caesar, it was the capital of Andalusia under the Visigoths, the head of its own caliphate under the Moors, and capital of Christian Spain under St Ferdinand. In biblical times it may have been Tarsis, sending King Solomon his ivory, apes and peacocks: and in the first years of Spain's transatlantic empire it was the sole entry-point (by law) for all the purloined wealth of the New World. It was then at its apogee, the New York of the Mediterranean, frantic, sophisticated and multifarious: in the words of an old Spanish saying, if you wanted pigeon's milk, Seville was the place to get it.

Later it acquired a different kind of reputation. For many northerners it became the most quintessentially typical city of all Spain. Figaro was born here, Don Juan prowled the narrow streets, and Carmen immortalized the tobacco factory and the bull-ring. Seville stood for intrigues conducted through wrought-iron grilles, for orange blossom and red roses, for love and music and death.

Well, the bull-ring and the tobacco factory still stand, although the latter is now the university (thereby exchanging, in the words of a recent wag, one kind of noxious weed for another). The city's squares are indeed fragrant with orange blossom in April, and in May the pavements are as blue as the sky with fallen jacaranda flowers. The towers of the churches, many of them old Moorish minarets, rise above the low roof-line like the Wren spires above eighteenth-century London (there were 140 of them when the French captured Seville in 1810 during the Peninsular War); and the Guadalquivir flows lazily below the Tower of Gold. But the river is silted (the cause of the city's decline over the last 250 years) and the churches are too far apart for easy walking. Much of the space between them is a dusty shambles of undistinguished houses that are not even whitewashed in the Andalusian manner, with an increasing record of street-crime. Taken as a whole, Seville is a disappointment.

The answer is not to take it as a whole, especially if you are short of time, but to concentrate on a selection of buildings, some of which have the added advantage of being clustered within walking distance of the cathedral. My own favourite starting point would not be the cathedral itself, but a chapel one-thousandth the

19

size. It lies half a kilometre south down the Avenida Queipo de Llano, on the north side of the big roundabout of the Plaza de Calvo Sotelo. It is the chapel of Maese Rodrigo, the only surviving building of the first university of Seville. It dates from the beginning of the sixteenth century, and incorporates a number of architectural features which will be recurring elsewhere throughout this book.

The entrance, easily overlooked, is a plain red-and-white gothic arch. The interior is a single small room, but all the details are rewarding. Many are in the Moorish style, although Ferdinand had recaptured the city from the Moors 250 years earlier. The nave ceiling, for instance, is a magnificent *artesonado*, and in so low a room the details are clearly visible. The tie-beams with their cross-over decoration are typical, as is the carving and gilding in the centre panels. The chancel roof has moved on to gothic: so have the handsome chancel arch and the decorative frieze that runs round the upper wall. Thus the embellishment of the building is divided between the styles of East and West.

But the styles also commingle. Around the gothic chancel, as well as around the nave, runs a dado that is pure Arab. It is made of multi-coloured Cuenca tiles, the forerunners of the modern tiling that decorates so many Andalusian halls and stairways.

Finally, the reredos. There are many such in Spain, often in a baroque style so punitively aggressive that the sensitive visitor shades his eyes and passes by. But this one is earlier in period, restrained in treatment and manageable in size. Its sixteen paintings are set in what is effectively a single divided frame, curiously flanged at top and sides, and delicately carved and gilt. It dates from 1520, and is the finest in Andalusia.

Leaving the chapel and strolling north, you come almost immediately to the Plaza del Triunfo. Ahead is the towering bulk of the cathedral. To the right, behind the rank of horse-drawn barouches which constitute the most agreeable (but expensive) way of touring the city, rise the towers and walls of the *alcázar*, traditionally founded by Julius Caesar and therefore one of the oldest continuously inhabited castles in the world.

These external fortifications are Almohad (built by the fanatical Moroccan sect who ruled southern Spain in the twelfth and thirteenth centuries), tempting the visitor to believe that this is an intact Arab palace. But the interior, including the finest Moorish-style decoration, dates from the Christian era. It was mostly built in the fourteenth century by Pedro the Cruel, an unlikeable gentleman whose fondness for things Moorish extended to wearing Arab dress, and to adopting the Moorish practice of pickling the heads of his enemies in salt and camphor. His sobriquet is attested by various monuments in Seville. In the monastery of San Isidoro, outside the city, is the tomb of a lady whom he burnt alive, and Maria Coronel Street is named after another who is said to have disfigured her own face with boiling doughnut-fat in order to repel his advances. His wife fared no better: he had her killed by one of his archers. Here in the *alcázar* itself he executed one of his half-brothers, and murdered a distinguished guest from Granada for the sake of his jewels, one of which was given to England's Black Prince in gratitude for military aid and later worn by Henry V at Agincourt. It ended up in the Imperial Crown of England. But Pedro had little time to enjoy his palace: within three years of completing it, he was stabbed to death by another half-brother.

Nevertheless, he succeeded in creating one of the architectural masterpieces of Andalusia. To do so he used craftsmen from Granada – the result of a lease-lend agreement – which is why parts of the *alcázar* are inferior only to the Alhambra. The entrance to the inner palace is a solemn sandstone rectangle that interrupts the surrounding colonnade. Its Moorish detailing is a foretaste of what lies within, and includes a characteristic mingling of East and West: a blue ceramic frieze of Cufic script proclaiming 'There is no conqueror but Allah', framed by a gothic inscription naming Pedro as the castle's constructor.

Inside the doorway is a vestibule, small and cool and dim, with a fine ceiling and chiselled plasterwork in aqueous shades of blue and green and white. Turn left

---

Moorish delicacy in a Christian palace: the Patio de las Doncellas in the *alcázar*, Seville.

through an elaborately decorated corridor, and you are in the Patio de las Doncellas, the heart and jewel of the palace.

If this is your first visit to Andalusia, you will already be gasping from the shock of being plunged into an alien element, an architecture fundamentally different from anything in northern Europe. Ceramic tiles form a bewilderingly flamboyant dado around every room and passageway, and around the patio itself. Above are the endlessly repeated and varied designs of the *sebka* plaster, covering every spare fragment of wall, inside and out. The inner chambers are reached through finely inlaid double doors: even the corbels that hold the door-pins are works of art.

One of these entrances leads into the Salon of Charles V, with a magnificent coffered ceiling. The next brings you to the famous Hall of the Ambassadors. This is a perfect cube surmounted by an intricate 'half-orange' dome. It is not large — most rooms in Moorish palaces are small — but the ceiling is high, and arches leading into the patio and into other rooms increase the impression of space. It is bare of furniture, which is as well given the riot of decoration which completely covers the walls and ceiling ... ceramic and mosaic tiles, carved stone and plaster and larchwood, painted panels and bosses and stalactites. Multi-coloured horseshoe arches rest on capitals dating from before AD 1000, and high on each wall are balconies (intrusive later additions) supported by dragons with gilded wings. Beneath your feet you are tempted to look for bloodstains, since this is where Pedro murdered his half-brother.

Nearby is the private sector of the palace, centred on the tiny three-storeyed Patio of the Dolls. While peering for the two curious miniature faces that give the place its name, spare a look at the capitals of the columns. They are ancient — some are pre-Moorish — and almost all are different.

The upstairs apartments, reached by an ornamental staircase in the corner of the *alcázar*'s main courtyard, are on the whole less interesting. Next to the staircase is the entrance to the Chamber of Commerce, founded by Ferdinand and Isabella to handle the new influx of trade from America. Beyond it is the chapel, a bare

Above **Originally, all the walls and ceilings of Moorish palaces were painted: now only the tiled dadoes retain their colour.**

Right **Embroidery in plaster: *sebka* work in the *alcázar*, Seville.**

room with a stone bench around it and an unusual roof, with brilliantly gilt rosettes and zig-zags instead of the normal mudejar coffers and tie-beams. Over the altar is a large flanged triptych, featuring the Virgen de los Navegantes, beneath whose protective cloak shelter a number of characters associated with the Indies, including Columbus, Vespucci and assorted monarchs.

Like all civilized people the Moors were gardeners, and their conquerors followed their example. The *alcázar*'s gardens are extensive and elaborate, an oasis of fountains, trees, box-hedges and scented air, threaded by almost a kilometre of paths. Stonework juts in scattered outcrops among the sea of foliage and rose-blossom — stairways and balusters, an early sixteenth-century archway, and the pavilion of Charles V, built in 1543 beside an orange tree said to

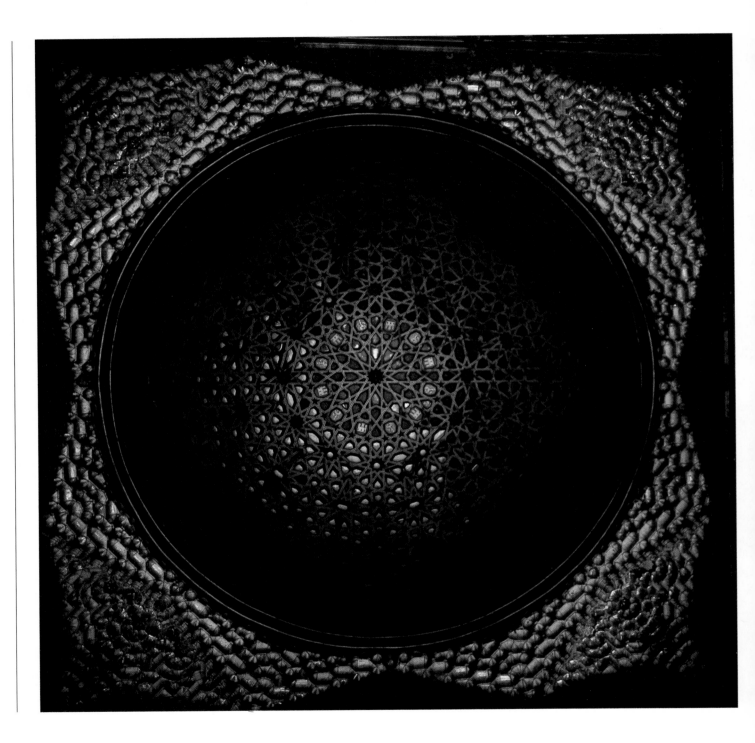

have been planted by Pedro himself. The Venetian ambassador to Charles' court called this the most peaceful spot in Spain.

On the other side of the castle wall to the east, a tranquillity of a different kind pervades the Santa Cruz quarter, the old Jewish ghetto of Seville. You can enter it through the archway at the far end of the large and gracious Patio de las Banderas, a miniature *plaza mayor* next to the *alcázar*. This brings you into the Calle Juderia, where the terracotta fortifications jut high overhead and flowers spill from window-boxes. A little further is the Plaza Doña Elvira, with flowerbeds and orange trees and a fountain. The area is full of squares like this, and many have outdoor restaurants, the pleasantest eating-places in Seville, apart from the occasional necessity to swat away a strolling guitar-player. The houses here are brilliantly whitewashed, with their details picked out in yellow-ochre (which was thought to give protection against witchcraft).

Look out for the Hospital de Venerables Sacerdotes, dating from 1675, with a sunken red-brick patio and frescoes in the church, notably on a dome by Valdés Leal (1630–91) like an inverted Sèvres sugar-bowl. Or simply wander at random through the alleyways, beneath blank white walls and wrought-iron window-grilles, and past doorways that lead into small leafy patios within. Above are flower-decked balconies and great elaborate lanterns, and ancient pillars prop the street-corners.

Looming over all this is the Giralda tower, the most famous monument in Seville, brandishing its huge elaborate belfry against the sky. Once the minaret of the mosque that preceded the cathedral, it symbolizes the history of Andalusia – a Catholic belfry on a Moorish tower on a Roman base. The main shaft, a great bare expanse of brick enlivened only by an earthenware version of *sebka* relief, has survived largely intact from the Moorish occupation. If it lacks elegance, it certainly radiates a massive arrogance, as

A pool in the *alcázar* gardens, Seville, reflecting the Arabs' traditional love of water.

A dome in the *alcázar*, Seville: Moorish craftsmanship in a Christian palace.

befitted the second-largest mosque in all Islam. Inside, instead of a staircase, is a ramp up which St Ferdinand rode his horse when he captured the city in 1248.

Below the Giralda is the cathedral, begun in 1402 and finished in 1506, the largest gothic church in the world. 'Let us build a church so great', cried its creators, 'that those who see it may take us for madmen.' And indeed the building is so great that touring the interior is conducive to a crick in the neck. The figures crowning the magnificent iron screens that front the two main sanctuaries are high overhead, and the great reredoses, with their intoxicating welter

25

Above Seville cathedral and the Giralda tower: Christianity's largest gothic church, on the site of Islam's second largest mosque.

Right When the temperature rises in Seville, four feet are better than two.

of grouped figures and gilt architecture (wrought by craftsmen from twenty-six nations), similarly extend upwards into the stratosphere. The handsomely carved choir-stalls are more or less at eye-level, but they are locked away. The chapels all around the shadowy aisles are accessible to those with night-vision, but are barely worth the furlong's stroll.

An alternative stroll, from the cathedral square half a kilometre or so to the west, brings you to the Hospital de la Caridad, completed in 1674. Its ochre patio is enlivened with blue-and-white panels of Dutch tiles showing scenes from the Old Testament, and there is a church containing paintings by Leal and Murillo. The latter's depiction of Moses striking the rock shows the prophet wearing a horned halo, the result of a confusion, some say, between the Hebrew words *keren*, shining, and *karan*, horned. Five other Murillos, one now in the National Gallery in London, were stolen from here by the French.

Five minutes' walk to the north is one of the main squares, the Plaza Nueva, and next to it the Plaza San Francisco, into which debouches the Calle Sierpes, a bustling pedestrian street that contains the most fashionable shops. Between the two plazas is the town hall: long and well-proportioned, its pilasters and friezes are encrusted with a fine exposition of the plateresque style.

The other sights of Seville are further afield. Down by the river are the bull-ring and the thirteenth-century Tower of Gold, one of the many places where Pedro probably did not keep his treasure. (Wherever it was, it was stolen by his Italian admiral while Pedro was away in Bordeaux drumming up help from the Black Prince.) Nor is it probable that St Ferdinand imprisoned a miser here, with the task of counting a vast hoard of gold, according to another legend: but you can check this out for yourself – hold your ear against the wall, and listen for the chink of coins, the groans of the miser, and the voice of his gaoler shouting 'Count, count'. In fact the tower's name derives from the gilt tiles on its roof, and it used to be one of a pair of towers with a chain stretched between them across the river, to protect the city.

Further north is the Fine Arts Museum, situated in the early seventeenth-century convent of Nuestra Señora de Gracia, and containing a handsome collection of works by Herrera, Zurbarán and Murillo. The soft romanticism of Murillo's late period (the third quarter of the seventeenth century) is a little sugary both in style and subject, but he is well represented here in Seville. The crescent moon under the Virgin's feet in some of his many *Immaculate Conceptions* was a well-established purity symbol for Our Lady, but it is something of a shock to see it in a country where the crescent moon of Islam had flourished for so long. One of his smallest and most charming paintings in the museum, the *Virgen de la Servilleta*, is said to have been requested as a souvenir by a lay brother in a convent where Murillo was working, and to have been painted on a napkin because the artist had run out of canvas.

In northern Seville are a number of other monuments, including various churches that show their Moorish antecedents. But the most interesting options are two private palaces. The Palacio de la Condesa de Lebrija (a taxi-ride to the north) is not open to the public, but negotiations through the handsome grille in the entrance hall can usually achieve a subsequent visit. While negotiating, look downwards. The marble floor that gleams so richly in the gloom is Roman, brought here in 1914 from the great city of Italica whose remains lie across the river. The colonnade surrounding the central patio is paved with more of this *opus sectile*, while in the middle is a huge mosaic, also from Italica. On every side are Roman artefacts, urns and basins, pillars and amphorae, sculptured busts and a well-head. More mosaics pave the rooms behind the main patio: one features a lion, a tiger and a panther – typical of the beasts that fought the gladiators in Italica's huge amphitheatre. There are garden patios at the back, and over the staircase is a fine *artesonado* ceiling from a palace at Marchena. Everything in this building is richly satisfying, providing you overlook the fact that it all came from somewhere else.

Twentieth-century exuberance in the Plaza de España, Seville.

Many of the materials for Pilate's House, too, were imported, but the palace was specially built to accommodate them. It was begun in 1480 and finished a generation later: a copy, according to tradition, of the Praetorium, Pontius Pilate's headquarters in Jerusalem. The result is a heady blend of the Moorish, gothic and renaissance styles, stupendously ornate, but proportioned on a scale modest enough to permit you to imagine, with a flash of envious fancy, that you might live there yourself.

It lies a kilometre east of the Lebrija palace. As with so many Moorish-style buildings, the exterior is unassuming, a bare brick wall at a bend in the street: the only elaboration is the Italianate marble gateway of 1533. Across a courtyard, through an arch with finely wrought iron gates, is the two-storey patio on which the house is centred. It manages to feel both simple and grand, and both eastern and western, with *sebka* work below and Roman-style terracotta above. The inner rooms give off it on each side.

The palace's air of transcendent luxury derives from the ceilings and the wall-tiles. Indoors, both look a little heavy and gloomy, but out here in the patio the tiles can be seen at their best. They are the finest in Spain, in dark bruised colours, and form the usual dado all around the building. Above one corner of the patio are tiles of a different kind – the blue-and-white roof-tiles that cap the stubby tower over the staircase.

The chamber on the right contains one of the best ceilings, a mixture of renaissance coffering with Moorish stalactites, and of western coats of arms with eastern inlay work. The window-shutters are exceptionally fine mudejar carpentry, and beyond them is the garden. To step out into it is to appreciate the Arabs' genius for combining architecture and horticulture. In the shade of an immense jacaranda tree fountains splash and birds sing, and rambler roses climb up palm trees in an exuberant commingling of Europe and Africa. On the other side of the house is another larger garden, so that the palace lies in a lush jungle, whose bright colours beckon through the exterior grilles of the sombre salons.

The upper floor is partly assigned to an unexceptional small museum, but the staircase up to it is worth the climb, or at least a startled look from below. It is capped by an elaborate half-orange vault similar to that over the Hall of the Ambassadors at the *alcázar*, and the surrounding stretches of ceiling have stalactite bosses that point downwards with an arrogance that verges on menace. Coloured tiles are everywhere. Set among them, at the top of the stair, is a copy of Murillo's *Virgen de la Servilleta*. Although Virgin and tiles both originated in the same part of the world, they are uneasy companions here, as is so much else in this riotously eclectic building.

But for many visitors the most thrilling and colourful of Seville's spectacles is not executed in stone or tile or precious metal. It is the world-famous celebration of Holy Week. All other activities are paralysed and all hotels full, which makes this a difficult time for visiting the city, and the rituals proceed at a very Spanish tempo: but as a spectacle of colour and theatricality and passionate Catholicism it is unique. Each night, for hours, the processions wend through the streets with a solemnity enhanced by the variety of costumes, military, secular and religious. The most striking are the all-enveloping cloaks, in different patterns, of the various church lodges: their first appearance in the half-lit gloom causes an instinctive tightening of the stomach, since the tall pointed hoods with their menacing black eye-slits have been adopted as the uniform of the Ku Klux Klan.

Amongst the vari-coloured eddies of human participants ride the great floats, like galleons above a fleet of small craft. Carried by thirty or forty sweating porters, they are half-tonne concoctions of gilded wood and plaster and encrusted vestments, topped with statues of the Saviour, the Virgin and appropriate saints, many of them carved by the great sculptors of the seventeenth century. Lurching and bobbing to the slow-march gait of their bearers, these tall figures assume an almost human motion, and in the narrower alleys appear to be conversing with the watchers who crowd the balconies. At ground level children run between the phalanxes of marchers, flares blaze and drums beat out the rhythm. Sometimes the processions are interrupted by chanting – the high, cascading notes of a solo voice – or by dancing. At other times the porters

The chapel of San Jose in Seville, north of the central
Plaza Nueva. It has a very elaborate rococo interior.

lay down their burdens and repair to a bar for beer or hot chocolate. The destination of each cortege is the cathedral, where the holy figures are laid down and blessed.

This tremendous celebration is not all that Seville has to offer in the way of mass festivity. A week or two later the population regathers, swelled by visitors from across all Andalusia, for the Spring Fair. This is held in a park outside the city. At one end is a giant fun-fair, with stalls and rides and ferris wheels which could be found anywhere in the world. At the other end is a scene which is only found here. This part of the park is divided by a grid of sandy boulevards, along which are pitched continuous rows of small marquees, each fronted like a chalet with a small fenced enclosure. The boulevards are decked overhead with hundreds of thousand of pink-and-white lanterns which are renewed every year.

Beneath the lanterns, by day, there passes a continuous cavalcade of horsemen and horse-drawn carriages. The high-stepping horses shine in the spring sunlight, and their manes and tails are plaited with coloured ribbons. The riders sport flat hats, black waistcoats and trousers, and haughty expressions. Seated side-saddle behind them, or lounging elegantly in the open landaus, are women in the vivid ice-cream colours of Andalusian dress, with layered skirts whose flounces cascade down the flanks of the horses, or froth up like great bouquets of flowers in the carriages. The leather chaps worn by many of the horsemen provide a Wild West touch, as do the hitching-rails outside the marquees, to which the horses are tethered while their riders, erect in the saddle, manipulate tall thin glasses of fino, the dry sherry which is the only wine publicly drunk in these parts. Further bottles of it clink in readiness on the velvet cushions of the landaus, and the counters in the tented bars dispense it in a mighty flood: never by the glass, always by the bottle.

As dusk falls, the horses and carriages depart, but the pedestrians throng ever thicker, and the endless skeins of lanterns illuminate the boulevards with a sepia glow. The marquees are crowded. Their canvas fronts are rolled up, and inside each is a marionette show of figures in perpetual motion. From now until past dawn the people dance, and the most enduring sound of Seville – the sound that those who hear it never forget – is the rhythmic clapping of hands. It continues, with short intermissions during the morning hours, for a week.

The choice of places to visit outside Seville is limited less by any architectural deficiency than by the terrain. Scenically, this is the least dramatic corner of Andalusia. To the north lies the Sierra Morena, but it is blandly benign compared with the mountains further east. Nevertheless it offers cooler air than the city, and a pleasant drive can be made north-west, through rolling cork woods, eucalyptus groves and meadows where fighting bulls graze in preparation for their final hour in the Seville bull-ring, to the pleasant hilltown of Aracena. There are good restaurants here, and the surrounding area fancies itself as something of a gastronomic centre. The *pata negra* pigs that graze the acorns make good pork and ham and salami, and there is local lamb (not commonly available in Andalusia), together with game such as hare, partridge and pigeon. Further south the meadows produce mushrooms, white truffles and other edible fungi.

Above Aracena stands a ruined twelfth-century castle, partly rebuilt a century later by the Templars, who also built a church with a fine tower and doorway on the site of the former mosque. Underneath, snaking into the roots of the hill, is the Gruta de las Maravillas, a cave whose glittering stalactite roofs, stained with the many colours of the pervading minerals, recall a distant echo of Pilate's House. Nature holding the mirror up to art.

Closer to Seville, in the same direction as Aracena, there is another place which is worth a visit. This is the great Roman city of Italica. After crossing the Guadalquivir, turn north following signs to Merida. Italica is on a loop road to the left, clearly signposted. It was founded in 206 BC by Scipio Africanus as a settlement for his veteranś, and claims to have been the birthplace of three emperors: Trajan, Hadrian and Theodosius. Its ruins extend for 10 kilometres, and it flourished for more than 500 years until the Visigoths picked the nearby village of Hispalis for their capital. Hispalis became Seville, and Italica became a stone-quarry.

Little now remains. What justifies the visit is the amphitheatre, and some fine mosaic floors. The former is immense, and it is hard to believe that cornfields grew over it for centuries. The surviving rows of seats are missing their top 12 metres, but they are still a formidable testimony to Roman engineering and to the exigencies of crowd control. Above, the ruptured blocks of grey ashlar look like the product of a titanic earthquake, but beneath them is an elaborate warren of barrel-vaulted galleries which open up onto countless stairways, bright with poppies. In the centre of the arena, which offered spectacles for 40,000 onlookers, are the approach tunnels which permitted the gladiators and beasts and other performers to reach the stage.

A short distance away up the sloping hillside is the site of the residential district of the rich, on the crown of the hill to catch the breezes (the plebs lived further down towards the plain). The mansions up here were spacious, as the extensive mosaic floors illustrate. Most of the designs are geometric, but some show figures . . . men hunting ostriches, crocodiles, horses with tails, and a spider apparently wearing a bishop's mitre. A series of colourful birds whets your appetite for any further treasures that still lie under the dusty scrub. Only a fraction of the site has been excavated. Two bathhouses and a forum are still being restored, and the theatre (a disappointment) lies over a kilometre away among modern houses.

The first stop on a tour of the Guadalquivir delta, Sanlucar la Mayor, was also a Roman town. It has two interesting churches. San Pedro dates from the twelfth century and is hard to find, tucked away on the south side of the town behind the remains of a castle. Its exterior has a defensive look: inside, a monumental stair leads up to three altars. The slender tile-capped tower, formerly a minaret, stands 15 metres away. Santa Maria, another converted mosque, is larger, and stands beside a little square where there is a bar – an important landmark during the thirsty months. Dating from the thirteenth century, its architecture is a lively mixture of Moorish and gothic, as typified by the Arab frames surrounding the lancet windows on the west front. Inside are plain gothic arches on round pillars, a ceiling in the *artesonado* style (but eighteenth-century), and a sanctuary with Roman columns and capitals built into its walls. The massive tower has a ramp running up inside instead of a stair, as in the Giralda.

From Sanlucar head south over the motorway to Benacazon and Aznalcazar. There is no great need, at this stage of the journey, to peer too devotedly through the car windows. The villages are drab and the landscape flat and featureless. Andalusia will be better than this. At Pilas you can carry on to Almonte, beyond which are the rolling vineyards of the Condado district. At the end of September there are wine festivals at Bollullos and La Palma del Condado, and various cellars can be visited. The wines are white and mostly fortified for drinking as aperitifs or with dessert. Columbus took Condado wine to America, but today it is undistinguished stuff.

Alternatively, turn south to Villamanrique de la Condesa. This boasts a palace with a patio as elegant as any in Seville or Cordoba, and a garden that blooms like Eden in the dusty plain. It belongs to a member of the Royal Family, which makes access problematical – but means that the road to the little village is velvet-smooth. Not so the road onwards, although it is adequate. Unmarked on most maps, it leads through forests of umbrella pines directly to our destination, El Rocio.

As a village, El Rocio is a nonentity in the middle of nowhere. But for three days each year, at Whitsun, it is the scene of an astonishing pilgrimage, the origin of which lies back in the Middle Ages. A hunter, trudging the plains with his dog, found a statue of the Virgin hidden under a tree-stump, perhaps to protect her from the invading Moors many centuries before. The man brought her back in triumph to his home, but when he looked for her next morning she was gone. He found her back under the tree-stump. Twice more he failed to persuade her to leave. At last, in recognition of her obduracy, the local bishop ordered a shrine to be built around her. She has become known as La Paloma Blanca, the White Dove, and the shrine has become a big, garish white church.

Left The town hall at Almonte. Near here, in the thirteenth century, a shepherd found the miraculous Virgin now worshipped at the pilgrimage of El Rocio.

Above Deserted for most of the year, El Rocio is thronged with thousands of pilgrims during the Whitsun festival.

The rest of the village is a sprawl of low hovels. Normally most of them are empty and the population is numbered in dozens. But at the time of the pilgrimage the participants throng the countryside for a kilometre around. You must park the car and walk, through what has become a huge camp. Twenty years ago the pilgrims came in covered wagons decked with flowers, and on horseback, streaming in long convoys across the dry marshes and bivouacking each night to sing and dance around their camp-fires. Today most arrive by car, or in garlanded tractors, but still there are horses everywhere.

Strolling the wide streets between the single-storey shacks, you have the overpowering sensation of having strayed into a cowboy film. The streets are of sand and are crowded with horsemen, often, as at the Seville Fair, with girls pillioned behind them, their bright flounced dresses contributing to the nineteenth-century mood. Every house is as lively as a Dodge City bar, with music and dancing and horses hitched to the rail outside. If you walk slowly enough and look thirsty enough, you may be invited in for a glass or three of fino, and a bout of hand-clapping to accompany the singer of the moment.

Unlike the Seville fair, the main sound here is of drums. You can hear them beating as you approach the village. They are carried in the open wagons, or casually slung across the shoulders of men in the strolling groups. Another difference is that this is a peasant festival, and the beasts drawing the wagons or trotting down the streets are not high-stepping thoroughbreds but nags and mules. There are, however, many exceptions: there is no questioning the breeding of the grey mount of the flat-hatted, chap-wearing cavalier, who guides it through a series of elaborate caracols, round and round in the dust and to and fro, without spilling a drop from the glass of fino in his hand.

At night you find yourself in a different kind of film, perhaps a military epic. Camp-fires flicker among the rows of tents, and tethered horses snort and stamp. Long ranks of pilgrims form up in the darkness, and shuffle slowly through the streets to the beat of drum and fife, following the banners of the church lodges.

Hand-held candles illuminate the dark faces, and flares send drifts of smoke across the processions, while rockets explode ceaselessly overhead. The processions culminate in the square in front of the church. The banners are carried up on to a high platform, and the great crowd, standing shoulder-to-shoulder in the gloom, intones the responses of the Mass. Afterwards the bells clang out, and the White Dove herself emerges from her floodlit church, borne above the crowd on a float like a gilded bird-cage, and processes around the town. The celebrants surge forward to see her, and fireworks light up the sky.

Adjoining El Rocio to the south-east is the other major reason for visiting this region: the Coto Doñana National Park. It is the largest and most important in Spain, covering 50,000 hectares, with a further 26,000 protected around it. Running down to the coast and across to the mouth of the Guadalquivir, it offers a variety of terrain . . . shifting sand-dunes behind the shore . . . flat dry scrub with the breadth and bareness of the Serengeti Plains . . . and the marshes of the river delta, which, alas, are being increasingly drained for cultivation. One of the last great wildernesses of Europe, the Doñana has been eroded by the farmers from the north and the tourists from the south.

Its name derives from Doña Ana, wife of the 7th Duke of Medina Sidonia, who built a palace here in the sixteenth century. Her husband, who has achieved an ambivalent fame as the commander of the Armada (many ships of which were built with timber from the park) owned all this land – but the park predates him by three centuries. It was established in 1261 by Alfonso XI after the reconquest of Niebla (see p. 42), and became the favourite hunting-ground of the kings of Spain. When Philip IV came here in 1624, his supplies of comestibles make impressive reading: in addition to the already-famous hams of Aracena and other delicacies, he brought in snow every day from Ronda – 160 kilometres away – on the back of 46 mules. Doña Ana's palace was used as the hunters' base, and it still exists. It has been visited not merely by a succession of kings but also by Goya, who painted his *majas* here (the notorious pair of portraits, one clothed, one naked, said to have been modelled on the

Duchess of Alba). It was built, according to the American writer James Michener, from the ballast-stones of English ships trading in sherry.

Today, there are two ways of viewing the wildlife, depending on the time you have available: on foot, or by Land Rover. (Neither can be combined with a visit to the Whitsun festival at El Rocio. The presence of several thousand singing and drum-beating pilgrims is not conducive to game-stalking, and the park is closed.) The sectors which can be visited on foot are in fact outside the park, to the west of the road that leads down to the coast. No prior reservation is necessary and entrance is free. The first place you come to is just a kilometre south of El Rocio, on your right. This is the principal information centre, from which a 2-kilometre track leads to three hides overlooking the River Rocina. Between the hides are shady copses of umbrella pines and open hillocks of scrub. Or you can drive 7 kilometres further west to the Acebron Palace, a curious modern edifice containing an anthropological exhibition, whence shady paths lead through woods of cork oaks, willows and chestnuts, along the Rocina and beside a small lake.

Returning to the main road and continuing south for another 7 kilometres, you will find the Acebuche Reception Centre a little way off the road to your right. This offers another exhibition room, a coffee shop, and a footpath around the artificial Acebuche Lake. It is also the departure point for the four-hour Land Rover trips which are the only permitted way of driving through the park itself. These trips must be booked in advance by letter or telephone.

The scenery alternates between the very dry and the very wet. What you are likely to see in the way of wildlife will depend, as ever, on luck, the time of day, and the time of year. Spring and autumn are the best seasons for viewing over 250 species of birds. The Doñana specialities include the purple gallinule (look for them on the Rocina, when it is flooded), and a dozen pairs of imperial eagles. In the woodlands are hoopoes, crested tits and short-toed tree-creepers. Griffon vultures, marsh harriers, kites and other raptors are common enough for you to be unfortunate not to see a selection. And in the migration seasons of

spring and autumn the park is a staging-post for hundreds of thousands of waterfowl ... geese and duck and teal ... purple herons, storks, spoonbills and flamingoes. The latter are a favourite diet of the imperial eagle – and they know it: they have only to see one, to fold their wings and crash to the ground in panic. There are also several species of mammal, including lynxes, boars and wild-cats.

The only nearby accommodation is at Matalascañas, on the coast to the south. There is no other reason for visiting this gruesome modern agglomeration of hotels and villas – except for its situation. On either side stretches one of the finest and emptiest beaches in Europe, the so-called Costa de la Luz, which extends for over 350 kilometres from the Portuguese border to the Strait of Gibraltar.

It would be nice to enjoy these golden sands somewhere else – anywhere else – than at Matalascañas, but the fact is that this is almost impossible. Heading west towards Huelva, you find an endless belt of dunes between you and the sea, up to 15 metres high and seldom less than a kilometre or two wide. There are places where you could park your car and trek off through the soft sand, like a Foreign Legionnaire, but the only non-taxing access to the beach is at a turning just before Mazagon, 22 kilometres west, where there is a pleasant little parador set high above the sea (even here you have to walk down), in an African-looking garden among pine trees. Previously there have been two turnings, marked Torre del Oro and Fontanilla, but both involve a walk at the end.

Finally, the side-road to the little port of Mazagon itself leads to a road that runs for a few kilometres along the shore, between villas old and new which fence off the sea. There are no hotels, bars, restaurants or hostels – though this is changing – and access to the beach is infrequent. It is a frustrating experience to stand beside the harbour and see the shoreline curving away to the left beneath its sandy cliffs, shining and solitary and unattainable.

Driving on towards Huelva you need to roll up the windows and refrain from inhaling, as petro-chemical developments sprawl across the landscape. After 11 kilometres turn right towards Palos and Moguer, for

the first of three places connected with Christopher Columbus. This is the Franciscan monastery of La Rabida, which is soon signposted on your left. It stands on a knoll above the estuary of the Rio Tinto, surrounded by eucalyptus trees, a leafy refuge among the industrial horrors. It was here that Columbus arrived in 1491. His plans to reach the East Indies by sailing west had been rejected, perhaps understandably, by Isabella and her advisers, and in despair he was heading down the Tinto to Huelva, en route for France, where he was hoping for a better reception of his schemes. But the prior of La Rabida had more vision than the queen. He took in the wild-eyed mariner and his little son, and being the queen's confessor he persuaded her to authorize Columbus's voyage.

A tall commemorative column overlooks the driveway that runs through flowerbeds and palm trees to the front door of the monastery, which dates from the fourteenth century but was restored in 1892. Columbus lodged here, in a room over the mudejar patio, and various objects connected with him are exhibited, including the thirteenth-century Virgin from Palos before which he knelt to obtain benediction for his voyage, and a fourteenth-century processional cross. And there is a document, recently discovered and of huge patriotic importance, which is claimed to prove that the great explorer, commonly supposed to be Genoese, was really Spanish.

Palos, a few kilometres further on, is a seedy little town, yet it was the port from which Columbus set sail with his three tiny caravels on 3 August 1492, and to which he returned the following March. His second voyage also started here, and it was here that Cortez landed in 1528 after conquering Mexico. Seldom can such an unprepossessing settlement have been associated with such momentous events. The church of San Jorge was built in 1473, and so was new when Columbus prayed here. Storks nest in the tower with its traces of blue-tile banding. The interior is pleasingly plain, with brick gothic arches and a somewhat

The monastery of La Rabida, at the mouth of the Rio Tinto. Here Columbus found the first sympathetic hearing for his schemes.

restored *artesonado* roof. Beside the altar and over the fifteenth-century crucifix with its slim but muscular Christ are the remains of wall-paintings, one of the patron saint, the dragon-slayer, and another of St James, the Moor-slayer, patron saint of Christian warriors. There is an iron pulpit from which the royal authority for Columbus's expedition is said to have been proclaimed: now without steps, it hangs incongruously on the wall like a tin parrot cage. Next to the church is the little square where two local citizens, the brothers Pinzón, helped Columbus recruit crews for the *Niña* and the *Pinta*, which accompanied the *Santa Maria*: and a hundred metres to the east is the fountain, now spankingly renovated and far from the sea, where the expedition filled the water-casks that lasted them to America.

Another 7 kilometres, and another plain little town, Moguer. Its church, with an elaborate Giralda-like

Andalusia has some of the most unspoilt coastline in Europe.

tower, is hardly worth searching for: but on its northern outskirts is one of the most rewarding complexes of buildings in Andalusia, the convent of Santa Clara, founded in 1348. Seldom visited, and barely mentioned in the guidebooks, it boasts a remarkably complete and well-preserved set of residential and ecclesiastical rooms: and being unoccupied it is not *in clausura*, like so many other monasteries and convents, and can be seen in its entirety. The overall style is serene, plain, almost severe, partly because all the brickwork was whitewashed in the eighteenth century, to exterminate a plague of insects.

On the left of the long exterior façade is a gateway into a small yard. Here you must seek the custodienne who will show you round. Adjoining the main patio is a dormitory. This too is whitewashed, with little decoration except an *artesonado* roof and traces of wall-paintings, and lit by tiny lancet windows. What makes you catch your breath as you enter is its size. In a land of small rooms it is immense – nearly 50 metres long. Pedro the Cruel had nothing like this. It dates from 1509 and there is a similar room above: the nuns slept downstairs in summer and upstairs in winter.

Ahead of you is a series of further rooms, including a meeting-room, a plain sixteenth-century refectory with benches down the side, the sixteenth-century *antecoro* with another *artesonado* roof, and finally the church. This contains two remarkable treasures. First, there is a unique set of fourteenth-century choir-stalls, carved and painted, with a lion at each nun's elbow, elaborate columns between each seat, and the coats of arms of the Portocarrero family who founded the convent. In front of the altar are the Portocarreros themselves, five of them side by side, carved in exquisite alabaster that shines in the half-light. Columbus often prayed in this church and gave thanks here after his first voyage. He could not have picked a better place.

From Moguer you turn north and cross the noxious Rio Tinto, familiar to readers of the financial pages. (It

The convent of Santa Clara, one of the most completely preserved religious complexes in Andalusia.

truly is *tinto*, or red.) Ahead, the road continues up into the Sierra Morena and on to Aracena: but if you are now returning to Seville you must turn east onto the N431. After 15 kilometres you reach our last stopping-point on this circuit, the little town of Niebla. Its site is unremarkable, tucked beside the railway line and the scummy, metallic waters of the river, yet this is a place with a long and noble history, to which various relics still attest. Niebla was the Roman Ilipula, and Scipio defeated the Lusitanians near here in 206 BC. The Visigoths made it the head of an episcopal see, and the Arabs the head of an independent state. Today it boasts the only complete town-wall in Spain, with 46 towers: smaller and less magnificent than the famous fortifications of Avila, but more intimate and deserted. Nobody comes to Niebla.

From outside, the wall and its gates are all that is visible, since the houses inside are low. Drive past the left side of the old town until you see a belfry on your right, where you can turn in through a hole in the wall. Beside you as you enter is the Puerta de Socorro, with a well-preserved Moorish arch and guardroom, and a dog-legged entry – a common military device. Inside is the ruined church of San Martin, beside a little square. The town is small enough to stroll through on foot, or you can turn right inside the gate and drive along the inside of the wall. Turning slowly anti-clockwise you soon come to the Ox Gate, the Puerta del Buey, with another fine vaulted guardroom, standing a little outside the wall, and then, a couple of blocks further on, to the Water Gate. If, as its name implies, this is where the women used to draw water for the town, the townsfolk of those days must have had stronger stomachs or a purer river.

Beyond the Water Gate the road broadens into a long narrow square, with a bar on the right and on the left the ancient church of Santa Maria de la Granada, partly dating from the tenth century. The tower, which stands separate, is a virtually intact minaret, without the usual addition of a Christian belfry. The exterior of the church, a nesting-place for kestrels, is picturesquely built of alternate courses of brick and stone, with heavy overhanging eaves and roofs that jut at strange angles. On the north side is the former

Left Nor any drop to drink: the ore-sullied waters of the Rio Tinto near Niebla.

Above Niebla, sleeping off the weariness of its long history.

Road to nowhere: a farm on the plain beneath Carmona, where the Romans under Scipio defeated the Carthaginians and Numidians in 206 BC.

orangery of the mosque, a tiny irregular courtyard with Arab arcading on old columns. Inside the church is the familiar mixture of Muslim and Christian, with a gothic nave, blind Arab arcading on the north wall and a strange *mihrab*-like recess on the south. There is an earlier relic too – a Visigothic arch leading into a side chapel.

There is nothing else of architectural interest in Niebla (the hospital of Nuestra Señora de los Angeles has virtually disappeared), except for the ruins of the castle to the east, and the east gate, the Puerta de Sevilla. This fourth gateway confirms the symmetry of the original ground-plan – derived from that of a Roman camp – and hence its antiquity. This aura of history is very appealing, as is the extreme simplicity of the old town. To me, Niebla is like a miniature reliquary, of which the decoration is fine but worn with age, and which when opened reveals scant but intriguing traces of what it once contained.

In fact one of its finest treasures lies outside. As you leave the town on the road to Seville you cross a remarkably well-preserved Roman bridge, which spans the Rio Tinto on massively bulbous piers, symbolizing the solidity and confidence of the Roman presence in Spain.

There is another Roman settlement on the far side of Seville, 38 kilometres to the east, and as it contains a magnificent parador it offers an alternative source of accommodation to Seville itself. This is the little town of Carmona, and it is a jewel. It can be reached direct on the Cordoba road, or via Alcala de Guadaira to the south, where a large and spectacular castle was built by the Moors, above the bends of the River Guadaira. It was captured by St Ferdinand in 1246, and later used by Pedro the Cruel as a prison. One of the inmates, a relative of Pedro's mistress, sent messages for help from his dungeon, written in his blood and tied to the tails of rats. While you are scrambling around the walls and towers and keep, do not leave your car parked unattended in the romantically deserted little park outside the gate. It will very likely be robbed.

Whichever way you come to Carmona, stop first at the Roman necropolis outside the town to the west, north of the Seville road. You can park by the entrance, where there is an attendant to keep an eye on the car, and the little museum inside will provide you with a guide. The necropolis covers a low knoll, with prickly pears and irises sprouting in the rough ground between the tombs and walkways. It dates from around the birth of Christ, although some of the pots in the museum are six or seven hundred years older, showing that Carmona was an important settlement long before the Romans. (As is indicated by its name: any town name with the prefix *Car* is Iberian – unless it is *Cart*, which derives from the Phoenicians of Carthage.) Excavations here only began in 1881, since when about 300 tombs have been opened, with nearly another 500 still to be excavated (as has an amphitheatre on the other side of the road). The tombs are all hidden underground – the place looks like a rabbit-warren – except in cases where the roof has fallen in. Each is approached by a vertical shaft, which leads to a vaulted chamber, or a group of them, carved from the rock. Each chamber is a funerary filing-system, with stone receptacles holding the ashes of the dead in small round-topped recesses in the walls. It is quite disconcerting to peer into these recesses. In most of them the little boxes are still there, each with its neatly-fitting lid.

The biggest tomb, known as the Tomb of Servilia, is the size of a Roman villa, with a double portico surrounding an open patio. Despite its scale, it contains but a single tomb, evidently a much-mourned daughter of a wealthy family. Her vaulted burial chamber, together with the Tomb of Postumio, are now the only ones to reveal traces of the wall-paintings which earlier guidebooks refer to as a wealth of Pompeii-like frescoes. Alas, time has moved on, and the bright flowers and fruit and birds have faded from sight. Perhaps new explorations will resurrect new delights.

The first sight of Carmona itself is spectacular. Aggressively blocking your way is one of the finest and oldest fortified town entrances in Andalusia: the Alcázar de Abajo, the Lower Fortress, Moorish on Roman foundations, with the Seville Gate beside it. It may tickle the fancy to picture Julius Caesar superintending the laying of the massive blocks that form its base, since it was he who first walled the town, as he did Seville. But in fact the present layout is probably a couple of centuries later. It lacks the medieval sophistication of the dog-leg at Niebla, and the double horseshoe arch added by the Moors leads straight into a long barrel-vaulted guardroom, now open to the sky. High above you, the upper works of the Moorish castle add to the aura of impregnability: whenever this town changed hands, it was not by assault but through treachery or surrender.

The town itself lives up to the promise of its exterior, and is small enough to tour on foot. Inside the gate, take the right-hand fork up the hill, and you will soon see on your left the well-worn brick gothic door of San Bartolome. The great sandstone tower, with its belfry surrounded by a thicket of urns, shows well above the white façades of the surrounding streets. The church's interior is gothic, with brick arches and a vaulted stone roof.

Bear left at an attractive eighteenth-century house, with a baroque doorway and the remains of paintings on the walls, and after a couple of hundred metres you will find a pair of entrances on your right which lead into the market. This was formerly the convent of Santa Catalina, which explains its architectural elegance – a large and perfect brick-paved patio surrounded with white arches, banded in red, with blue-and-white ceramic urns on a parapet above. This dainty frame is filled with the colours and bustle of a typical Spanish market. The arcades, and sometimes the whole square, are crammed with stalls offering a cornucopia of fruit and vegetables, sacks of pulses and spices that recall a North African souk, and a jumble of clothes, brooms and other household impedimenta.

Return to the street and turn left almost immediately into the square called after St Ferdinand, who took the town in 1247. There is a bar here, and benches outside under the palm trees where you can sit and admire the varied assortment of sixteenth- and seventeenth-century buildings around you, some arcaded, some painted and some tiled. One of these, on the corner where you entered the square, is the town hall. The patio inside is modern, but it contains a fine Roman mosaic, black-and-white with five coloured heads, including that of Medusa in the centre.

Uphill from the town hall is the church of San Salvador. Dating from 1700, it has a florid baroque north door and, unusually, an east door, all in golden stone. One of the delights of Carmona is the contrast between the brilliant whitewash of the little dwellings that line the streets and the warm rich masonry of the churches and palaces.

Turn left out of the little square at San Salvador's east end, and then right, and you are soon in front of the big brick south side of Santa Maria, dating from the fifteenth century. At the church's south-east corner is the narrow façade of the Palace of the Marqués de las Torres, with a neo-classical doorway of 1755: and to the left, opposite the west end of the church, is the longer sweep of the Rueda Palace, in a similar style. High above is the church's fine multi-tiered tower, with glinting flecks of blue tile and a blue-and-white spire at the summit. The colour blue is an old Arab

Above **Carmona, Roman staging-post on the road from Cordoba to Seville.**

Right **Early seventeenth-century tiles in the square called after St Ferdinand, Carmona.**

antidote against the Evil Eye; the subsequent Christian builders, hedging their bets, made free use of it on their churches.

The entrance to Santa Maria is round the other side. The custodienne's window is high on the wall to the right, and it requires a good carrying voice or a deft aim with a handful of gravel to rouse her, if the church is shut. But the effort is worth it. Inside the doorway is a tiny patio, originally the orangery (or part of it) of the mosque which preceded the church. The surviving horseshoe arches rest on older pillars purloined from elsewhere, one of which is Visigothic with an engraved *calendario*, or list of saints' days. The inside of the church is elegantly gothic, with fine vaulting high overhead, and the seventeenth-century choir-stalls are handsomely carved.

Continuing towards the far end of town, you are on the Roman Via Augusta, which runs the length of Carmona from the Seville Gate to the Cordoba Gate. This is a picturesque walk, along a cobbled street with no pavements. Carmona is a true mix of typical Andalusian elements – white walls, black window-grilles, and russet roofs. All that is missing here is the blaze of flowers in pots which enriches so many of the villages.

At various points hereabouts you can cut through to the right and follow signs to the parador, which occupies the highest point of the town, inside the walls of the upper castle. This was originally Moorish, but as in the case of the *alcázar* at Seville, it was elaborated by our old friend Pedro the Cruel. It seems a little profligate to have built another palace so near his urban masterpiece, especially as the climate is similar (think what a nice summer resort he could have had up at Aracena): but presumably Carmona was a conveniently adjacent repository for his mistresses, political prisoners, and that elusive and ultimately burgled treasure.

Much of the curtain wall remains, notably the gateway, which carries traces of painting, thought to be early gothic. Inside, the castle remains are occupied by a garden and the parador, which is mostly modern but sympathetically styled, and possesses the inestimable benefit, in summer, of a swimming-pool.

From here you can return to the main street via the mid fourteenth-century church of Santiago, with a blue-tiled steeple and a well-proportioned sanctuary. The Cordoba Gate lies a few metres down the hill to your right. Stroll through it and look back. As at the Seville Gate, the huge stones at its base are second-century Roman, and rise on either side to octagonal towers with crenellated Arab upper-works. What lies between the towers is much later, dating from 1668. Tall classical pillars and blind windows, topped with a formal pavilion, set off the round-topped gate. It is all in yellow stone, wedged into a gap in the hillside and flanked by sandstone cliffs of the same colour. Swifts circle overhead, as they do over all the old buildings of southern Spain.

Outside the gate the modern road curls away to the right, but the Via Augusta to Cordoba and the rest of the world ran straight down the hill, crossing the stream at the bottom on a little bridge (more easily reached today by driving down the main road). The five arches are still almost intact, except for the surface paving. Beyond it is the vastness of the Corbones plain, where Scipio Africanus, the founder of Italica, defeated the Carthaginians and Numidians in 206 BC, and broke their power in Iberia for good.

In summer the view from the Cordoba Gate is bare and hazy. But on a clear winter's day the whole of central Andalusia is laid out before you. Cordoba is 100 kilometres away to the north-east, and at a similar distance to the south rise the mountains which are so much more characteristic and spectacular than the flatlands through which we have journeyed so far: the peaks of the Sierra Margarita to the right, and sweeping round behind them the jumbled crags of the Serrania de Ronda. Due east, at nearly double the distance, you can sometimes glimpse the great ridge that leads up to the eternal snows of the Sierra Nevada. As you stand there, on this long-inhabited whaleback of golden rock, almost the whole of the rest of this book is made visible.

Carmona: the mid fourteenth-century church of Santiago.

49

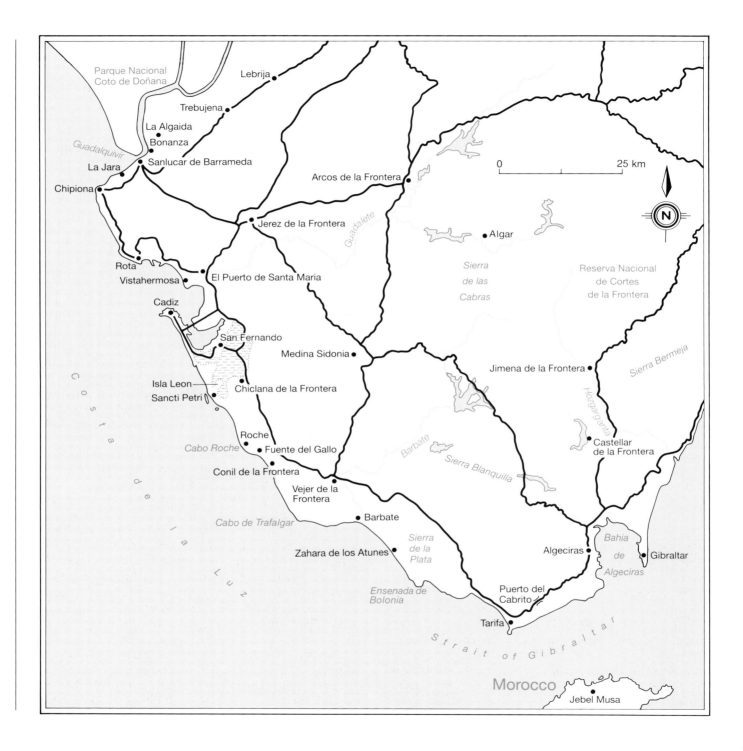

2
South to the Pillars of Hercules

Jerez – Sanlucar de Barrameda – Guadalquivir estuary –
Cadiz – Medina Sidonia – Vejer de la Frontera – Costa de la Luz –
Tarifa – Cape Trafalgar – the Pillars of Hercules –
Castellar de la Frontera – Jimena de la Frontera – Arcos de la Frontera

Not to be born would be best, or being born, to live at Cadiz.

Cyril Connolly

Cadiz province is off the main tourist beat, and its comparative isolation down at the southernmost tip of Andalusia, together with the emptiness of its breezy landscapes, gives the impression that history has passed it by. Nothing could be further from the truth. The mouth of the Guadalquivir has been a major entry-point to the heart of southern Spain since long before Christ, and the Strait of Gibraltar was bridged in 711 by the Moorish invasion. During the long campaign of the Reconquest, the province was the frontier between the Christians and the Moors, as is evidenced by the 'de la Frontera' suffix to so many of the local names. For 250 years the border towns were captured and recaptured, and their territories subjected to raid and counter-raid. The tales of chivalric derring-do and romantic love became one of the richest sectors of medieval literature.

Later, as the influence of Seville declined with the silting of the Guadalquivir, the ports near the river mouth, Sanlucar, Santa Maria and the ancient Cadiz, grew in wealth and were filled with palaces. Since then their bloom has faded again, and their husks are strewn along the Atlantic shore, withered but intriguing. Inland, the terrain gradually swells up from the marshes of the delta, and rolls out its fertile meadows until they lap up against the first of the great mountain ranges. Between the marshes and the meadows is a stretch where the soil glares blindingly white beneath the rows of vines that fill it. This soil and those grapes have made the fame and fortune of the town that stands in their midst.

Jerez de la Frontera, as its name implies, was much embattled during the war against the Moors, and it changed hands more than once. St Ferdinand captured it in 1251, but it was lost again by his son, despite a defence so gallant that the Moors had to drag the Christian commander, Garcí Gómez, from the walls with grappling irons (whereupon, impressed by his gallantry, they patched him up and restored him to his troops). Today it is an aristocratic but uninspiring little town, famous for wine and horses. It has a few interesting buildings, and these are conveniently assembled within walking distance of the big square just north of the castle, the Plaza de Arenal.

One block away to the east is the church of San Miguel, built on the site of a hermitage dedicated to the Archangel in thanks for his help in one of the battles against the Moors. Although the church dates from

The killing ground: on this rich plain east of Jerez 12,000 Moors routed 100,000 Visigoths and won Spain.

c.1430, the fine west façade is late seventeenth-century. Its classical pillars and pilasters are covered in plateresque decoration, and the filigree engraving gives the grey stone a curiously puckered look.

The interior is intriguingly varied, as though the builders thought it boring to design any of the half-dozen gothic bays the same. The vaults are all different. So are the piers, which when you reach the transept suddenly sprout decorative friezes in deep relief. The great reredos (1613–47) was the work of several distinguished craftsmen. The best known is Montañés (1568–1649), who contributed the figures of St Peter and St Paul, and the central reliefs showing the Battle of the Angels, the Transfiguration and the Ascension. Like his work elsewhere in Andalusia, these sculptures show Montañes' naturalistic and restrained style, particularly unusual in an artist of his period. Although the dividing pillars are baroque, the sombre tones of the gilding prevent any over-exuberance and create a mood of quiet majesty.

If you retrace your steps from San Miguel's west front, you will see a short way ahead the scant remains of the castle, or *alcázar* – a few stretches of wall, blank bastions pitted with swifts' nests, and an octagonal tower which may date from the Almohad period in the twelfth century. The masonry is not stone but brick, in flat tight layers, with a thread-bare look. The castle is closed, but you can walk round it to the left, past a statue of Alfonso the Wise, Ferdinand's son, he who lost the walls that now stand above him. Round the corner is a wide esplanade planted with palms and jacarandas, with a view over the plain that surrounds the town.

Beyond it is another terrace, studded with young citrus trees, which overlooks the formidable east end of the Collegiate Church, the town's cathedral. It stands, as so often, on the site of the previous mosque, and took 200 years to finish, from the late sixteenth to the late eighteenth centuries. The plain exterior is marred by disproportionately massive figures round the tall terracotta dome, and by the row of flying buttresses which may have been prompted by the great Lisbon earthquake of 1755. The interior is massive too, with plain renaissance arches resting on huge piers, in dark stone chequered with pale mortar. In the sacristy behind the altar are some second-rate paintings of the Zurbarán school. The former star of the show, Zurbarán's *Sleeping Virgin*, is now kept in the church's museum. Zurbarán's naturalism gives him a cutting edge in comparison with his younger contemporary Murillo, and this Virgin is unglamorously propped on her elbow, on a chair identical to those still hand-produced in small Spanish towns. But it is an early work (c.1625) and lacks the unsentimentality of his later style.

Returning outside and walking round to the west end, you will see a façade somewhat similar to that of

A bas-relief on the Collegiate Church in Jerez, which was begun in 1562 on the site of an earlier mosque, but not completed for 200 years.

The Virgin in glory, above the Plaza de la Asuncion, Jerez.

San Miguel, though less decorated. This is the most satisfying view of the church, since it is sited at the top of a massive (again, too massive) double staircase. The mudejar belfry is older and detached, a survivor from the mosque. At the bottom of the staircase is a little square, the scene of processions and dancing during the grape harvest festival, if you are here in September. A wine-press is set up, to which girls in Andalusian dress bring baskets of grapes for treading by the men. As the first juice of the year begins to flow it is solemnly blessed, and a cloud of white doves is released. For nearly a week there are cavalcades, flamenco dancing and bull-fights – for Jerez is famous for bulls, as well as for wine and horses.

Turning right out of this square, you will soon pass on the left the Palace of the Marqués of Bertemati, a gracefully proportioned building in a somewhat un-Spanish style, with big windows and elaborate door-ways. The cobbled street leads on to the pretty little Plaza de la Asuncion containing the former town hall, dating from 1575, a grand building in miniature. The renaissance façade is quaintly lop-sided, with an Italianate open loggia on the left. Inside is a fine library with over 25,000 books, some rare, and a small museum, of which the star exhibit is a Greek helmet from the seventh century BC, one of the few relics of the Greek presence in southern Spain.

At the far end of the square is the church of San Dionisio, founded in the thirteenth century by Alfonso the Wise but restored in 1728. It is tiny, and a charming Andalusian hotch-potch of styles. A minia-ture Moorish orangery precedes a gothic entrance, and the gothic arches inside are topped by a mudejar roof. Even the piers make the purist's head reel: intertwin-ing romanesque strands culminate in Moorish capitals. Outside the church to the north is the mid fifteenth-century Torre de la Atalaya, each side of which is decorated differently, with a blend of Moorish windows and gothic arches. As its name implies, this was once one of the watch-towers which are to be seen all over Andalusia, along the coasts and throughout the war zones, where they were used for sending smoke-signals across country from tower to tower.

You have now seen everything of interest within easy walking distance, and can reward yourself with a glass of fino at one of the bars that line the Plaza de la Arenal, only a short distance away down the street between San Dionisio and the old town hall. But there is a more distant place to see ... if you are male: the Carthusian monastery, La Cartuja, situated 5 kilo-metres out of Jerez on the C440 to Medina Sidonia (see p. 70). Nearby is the crossing of the River Guadalete which marks the battlefield where the Moors won Spain.

Founded in 1477 and now under restoration after many years of neglect, the Cartuja lies behind an imposing renaissance gateway, flanked with classical columns and decked with blue ceramic lozenges. No women are allowed beyond this point, and even males are forbidden entry to the monastery itself. Only the

Orange-scented shadows in Jerez.

Above **The September wine harvest is celebrated at the foot of these steps, beneath Jerez's Collegiate Church.**

Right **A detail from the convent of Siervas de Maria, Jerez.**

façade is visible: but this, dating from 1667, is one of the baroque masterpieces of southern Spain, a rich concoction of paired pillars and figures and ornamental urns surrounding a renaissance doorway and a recessed rose window, all in golden stone. Hidden within is a noble gothic cloister. Formerly there were many art treasures too, and a famous stud which has given its name to the Carthusian grey, said by some to be the forerunner of the Lippizaner of the Spanish Riding School in Vienna. But all was dispersed when the French arrived in the Peninsular War. Richard Ford, in his 1845 *Handbook for Spain* (essential reading for hispanophiles), noted that 'the loss of the horses will long be felt, when that of the friars is forgotten'.

Horses have remained part of the fabric of Jerez, together with its even more familiar product – wine. Both are displayed with typical Spanish flair. Visitors can enjoy an introduction to Spanish horsemanship at the Royal Andalusian Riding School in the Avenida Duque de Abrantes. It is situated in handsome gardens, and the display includes choreography dating from the seventeenth century, with music and costumes to match. This show is available throughout the year: but the main equestrian event in Jerez is the Horse Fair, celebrated for a fortnight in May. The connoisseur of horseflesh can admire the Carthusians and the Hispano-Anglo-Arabs, the result of cross-breeding between the thoroughbreds of the north and the original Arab and Barbary steeds of the invading Moors. There is also much horsemanship to admire. Jerez is the home of the *rejoneo*, the art of bull-fighting on horseback, which many visitors find more acceptable and spectacular than the normal bullfight. The action takes place at top speed, the bull has only one opponent and so is competing on more equal terms, and you feel that no harm is likely to come to the very expensive horse-flesh. There are a number of bull-fights during the fair, together with several riding competitions and displays.

General Primo de Rivera, dictator from 1923–30, was born in Jerez, and his statue in the Plaza Arenal commemorates his triumphs in the Moroccan war.

An entrance to the bull-ring in Jerez. The town maintains the art of the *rejoneo* – fighting bulls on horseback.

The main fairground lies on the edge of town, and you would be advised to visit it by taxi, if you can find one, since parking is difficult. The setting is a smaller-scale version of the Seville fair. The pavilions and illuminations are more modest, but this is compensated for by the splendour of the tall palm-trees and the wide sandy esplanades, and by the elegance of the participants. Here, the horses are even more sleekly aristocratic, and the horsemen, with their disengaged hands dangling at an angle so precise as to look carefully posed, are even more disdainfully erect in the saddle. And the women, lounging on the pillions amid the piled-up flounces of their dresses, are more . . . but no, no women could excel the women of Seville. The smell of dust and dung prickles in the nostrils, the sound of clapping fills the ears, and throughout the bustle the spirit of celebration and hospitality is never eclipsed: a cigarette-vendor urged me to put my *tapas* and bottle of fino among the wares on his table, and to wipe my hands on his tablecloth – 'it will be washed tomorrow'.

The fino I was drinking is Spain's most famous wine: in Hugh Johnson's words 'a paler wine, a cooler wine, a more druggingly delicious wine than you have ever tasted. It seems at the same time dry as dust and just teasingly sweet, so that you have to sip again to trace the suggestion of grapes.' Here in Jerez it is served as it should be – by the chilled half-bottle, so that it is always fresh. And here is where it is made. The great sherry houses are, for many foreigners, the main reason for visiting Jerez.

The word 'sherry' comes from Xeres (or Scheris in Arabic), the earlier spelling of Jerez, and when it first reached England in the sixteenth century the wine was known as sherris-sack, or plain sack, derived from the Spanish *seco*, meaning dry. Falstaff drank 'an intolerable deal' of it. In those days sack came from many places: Cyprus, Greece, Sicily and the Canary Islands. But the sack from Jerez became known as the best, partly through the help of Sir Francis Drake, who brought back 3000 butts of it when he attacked Cadiz in 1587. Two other nearby towns still produce sherry, Sanlucar de Barrameda and El Puerto de Santa Maria, but Jerez is the centre of the industry, which, as with the port and cognac businesses, is studded with the names of the English and Irish families who moved south in the seventeenth and eighteenth centuries: Byass, Osborne, Gordon, Sandeman, Terry, Williams, Garvey, Croft and Harvey.

The huge old *bodegas*, or wine sheds of Domecq, set in splendid gardens, are near the *alcázar* and Collegiate Church; those of Gonzalez Byass are nearby and others lie further north. Or, for anyone not otherwise planning to stop at Jerez, the Croft *bodega* is situated on the western bypass. This one is new (although the company was founded in 1678), but built in the traditional style. The process of making the wine is, like these buildings, a blend of old and new. The grapes, of the Palomino variety, are no longer trodden underfoot in the vineyards (with special cleated boots that crushed the fruit but not the pips), but pass through pneumatic presses here in Jerez. The vinification plant where this takes place is the modern part of the system. The wine ferments in tall stainless-steel cylinders, holding, in Croft's case, 7.5 million litres in all; and walking down the long aisles between them is like traversing a temple dedicated to high technology. But the buildings to which the wine passes four months later, clear as glass and fortified to 15°, are very different.

Stepping out of the glaring sunshine into one of the great *bodegas* where the sherry matures is to step back in time. As your eyes accustom themselves to the gloom, you realize you are in the company of maybe nine thousand oak barrels, stacked in rows four high, or sometimes higher. Many are made of wood 5 centimetres thick and are over a hundred years old: some are inscribed with the name of the type of sherry which they contain, or with the signatures of famous clients – generals, prime ministers, men of letters. The only illumination is from windows at the ends of the aisles, or set high up like clerestories. In this climate light means heat. Even the ground is kept as cool as possible: it is bare earth which is damped down every day.

Stainless-steel and oak make odd companions, but Jerez is not the only place to use them in juxtaposition. What *is* unique is the treatment of the wine in the barrel – the so-called *solera* system. The four layers of casks here in the *bodega* are of different seniorities: the newest at the top and the oldest at the bottom. As the wine is drawn off for bottling from the bottom layer – or rather partly drawn off, since the cask is left half full – the deficiency is made good from the next layer, which in turn is refilled from the layer above. Thus, unlike vintage wines, the sherry which is sold is a blend of many years' harvests, including some (since the bottom barrel is never drained) of considerable age. Just what kind of a blend depends, of course, on the house styles of the shipper and the skill of the blenders. A 9000-barrel *bodega* will be tended by just half a dozen men, who scramble like mountaineers among the great casks, day after day, tasting and comparing and syphoning the wine from one layer to another, and combining dozens of base wines to achieve the desired end-product.

As any sherry-drinker will know, the resulting blends are classified into various established types.

These vary from the dry finos – with a nutty bite that derives from the action of a strange local wine-yeast or *flor* – to the rich *olorosos*, which are dry in their natural state, but are normally sweetened-up for overseas markets. Indeed, the fact is that many export sherries bear little resemblance to what is drunk here in Jerez. Some or all of these varieties are offered for tasting daily at each of the big sherry houses, together with conducted tours of the premises.

If you drive out of Jerez to the north-west on the C440 you will traverse some of the vineyards where the sherry grapes grow. The soil glares white between the vines, and it is this chalkiness that achieves the unexpected delicacy in a grape that grows so far south and in such a heat. At the end of this road is another of the three sherry-towns, Sanlucar de Barrameda. Here too you can visit the *bodegas*, although the most characteristic end-product is somewhat different – a style of fino called a manzanilla, with a salty tang so subtle that it begins to vanish if the wine is moved, if only to Jerez. Thus the prime place to appreciate it is here in Sanlucar, and there is no better spot than the beach below the town, the Bajo de Guia.

Along the shore runs a narrow shabby esplanade, pullulating with people and redolent of fish. It is lined with *merenderos*, beach restaurants, where you can sip your manzanilla and look out at the estuary of the Guadalquivir. The muddiness of the water, the high stems and sterns of the fishing-boats moored there, and the flat scrubland on the far side all give a strangely African atmosphere to the view. But your meal will be pure Spanish. It is as though you have suddenly found yourself at the sharp end of that cornucopia which has been spewing out delicious fragments of sea-food across the counters of all the bars you have been visiting. Part of the appeal is the daintiness of the ingredients (the Spanish love diminutives, as is reflected by many of the word-endings in their speech): there are baby squid, anchovy fry smaller than whitebait, and sole the size of a child's palm: only the prawns are enormous, so that the restaurateur can call them langoustines and charge double.

That Congo-like shore opposite is a corner of the Coto Doñana nature reserve (see p. 36). Anyone unable

In Jerez, the Domecq family breeds wine, bulls and horses.

to make the long detour via Seville to the official entrance, or averse to taking guided tours, can catch a glimpse of the game – at least the winged representatives – by heading north from Sanlucar along the east side of the Guadalquivir estuary. Stay close to the river, on the country roads through Bonanza and La Algaida and on among the salt flats until you are opposite Lebrija, whence you can return via Trebujena. With luck you will see many of the waders and raptors that frequent the park across the river, including such curiosities as the pratincole which likes to lay its eggs on cow-pats.

Sanlucar itself is a neat, spry town of old two-storey houses with projecting balconies. Columbus sailed from here on his third voyage in 1498, and so did Magellan on his circumnavigation of the globe in 1519. Drive up the hill from the beach and park in front of the fourteenth-century church of Santa Maria. It has a fine multi-tiered tower of yellow stone banded with red, with blue tile decorations: and a splendidly diverse west doorway, with a gothic rose window above *sebka*-style stonework in a Moorish frame.

Inside, it is the Moorish elements that predominate. The Arabic tiles round the pillar-bases are modern, but there are antique examples in the chapel at the north-east corner. Over the nave and two aisles are exceptionally fine *artesonado* ceilings dating from 1363, carved and inlaid with patterns as bright as paint. Flanking the aggressively baroque choir is a unique feature – a pair of eighteenth-century galleries high on the wall, which were the private pews of the nobles who lived in the palaces on either side.

One of these buildings stands behind the west end of the church, its spanking white classical façade picked out with black window-grilles. This is the Palace of the Dukes of Medina Sidonia, the Guzmán family who were granted the town when it was recaptured in 1264. It can only be visited infrequently, but the mediocrity of the carvings and paintings within makes this no great loss.

More worthwhile is a stroll along the street to the right of the church tower. The houses here are low and trim, their façades black and white like the Medina Sidonia palace, and between them, covering several blocks, are the *bodegas* where the manzanilla is stored. After a few hundred metres you come to the fifteenth-century castle of St James. Like the other buildings it is low and pleasant, of shabby brick patched with stone, as yet largely unrestored. The biggest tower, a fine hexagon on the right-hand side, is bristly with weeds.

There is little else to see in Sanlucar, unless you are here in August, when there is a river festival. The festival queen arrives by boat from Seville, and there are bull-fights and flower-shows. As for swimming, the town beach does improve nearer the mouth of the river – to the left of the Bajo de Guia – but you would do better to continue down the coast to the south. At La Jara you can turn off through eucalyptus groves to a narrow beach with a bar, and at Chipiona is the Playa de Regla, a quiet resort of villas and low-rise hotels. Thereafter, there are signposts to a number of beaches set on a completely featureless piece of coast backed by vineyards and wheatfields. They are without charm – but also without people or commercial development. It is worth waiting for the last two, Candor and Costilla,

just short of the port of Rota: they are more crowded, but the shore here is lined with handsome pinewoods.

At Rota, the stalls and tiles in the church are worth seeing, but the town is notable for nothing else except the export of communion wine: so make a big loop round the American base and head straight for El Puerto de Santa Maria. Whether you stop here either is a moot point. This little fishing port is a strong contender for a drabness award. The narrow streets are mostly without architectural interest, the prioral church was clumsily rebuilt in the seventeenth century, and the fishing wharf is a stretch of concrete. Yet this was the Roman settlement of Menestheus, and a strong fortress under the Moors, from whom it was captured by Alfonso the Wise in 1264 (with the help of the Virgin Mary). Later, Columbus's voyages to the New World made the town rich, and it became known as the City of a Hundred Palaces.

Few of these glories remain. Today, Santa Maria is a *jolie laide*: without beauty or pretension. But she is robustly herself, and she offers the visitor three prime experiences: to see the castle with its remarkable mosque, to visit a sherry *bodega*, and to eat fish.

The fortress of San Marcos was once a Roman temple, then a Moorish stronghold, and subsequently the home of Columbus, as is attested by a plaque on the wall near the entrance. The present castle, built by Alfonso the Wise, is privately owned, but permission to visit it can be obtained from the police-station nearby.

It stands in the middle of town, small and neat, with a full array of dragon's-teeth merlons along its walls, and a narrow rim of garden between the outer and inner sectors. Although restored, there are still traces of original details. Outside, a curious russet frieze painted around the tops of the towers depicts Alfonso's arms, the towers of Castile and the lion of Leon, with a Latin text below. Inside are traces of Arabic inscriptions, and the castle's chief jewel, the mosque.

This tiny, dimly-lit room, with a low ceiling on two massive rows of piers, has the subterranean feeling of a crypt. Some of the thirty-three horseshoe arches rest on Roman columns, so that much of the history of the

Rota, traditionally a source of sacramental wine for England. The old name 'tent' wine derives from the Spanish *tinto*, or red.

town is encapsulated here. The *mihrab* is still intact, an ornate Moorish arch leading into a tiny vaulted chamber. Around it is a panel of decoration which at first sight looks like fresco, but is in fact a rare example of painted camel-leather. This technique was a Moorish speciality, but the motifs here evidently postdate the Moors, since they include a Christian fish and the words '*pax vobis*'. Other Christian additions include a pair of stained-glass windows, one of which depicts Alfonso, and the Chapel of the Sagrario on the north side. This boasts a handsome wrought-iron screen, whose gilt figures are cast in the round, unlike the flat-work which is a commoner style in Andalusia. Outside the mosque is another Moorish survivor — a tiny orangery. From here you can climb up on to the castle's flat roof and into its variously-shaped towers, the tallest of which was formerly the mosque's minaret: but the view is negligible.

However dusty the streets of Santa Maria, and however shrunken her former array of palaces, there is one aspect of the town which you will long remember. Down by the river-front, and in the side-streets, are a handful of restaurants. They are unprepossessing in appearance, and the best of them, on the corner of an old arcaded building, is the shabbiest and noisiest. Inside is bedlam, but there are also primitive tables outside under the arches. Next to the tables, opening onto the street, is a long gleaming counter laden with as glittering a galaxy of crustacea, as motley and outlandish a parade of fish and shellfish and components of shellfish, as you are ever likely to see. There are *pata rusa* and *boca rusa*, lobster legs and lobster claws. There are langoustines and langoustine claws and langoustine tails, together with mini-claws from some more exiguous relative. There are prawns and king prawns. There are goose-barnacles and cockles and other nameless shellfish. There are *necoras* and *cangrejos*, which are small crabs, and there are *buey mar* — sea oxen — which are big crabs. Antennae twitch fitfully above the gleaming beds of ice, and the smell is the smell of the sea.

You can take your pick of these riches, or you can sit at a table and order from a metre-long menu, washing down your choice with white wine from Arcos (see p. 82). The locals, however, opt for beer. Thronging the tables around you, they chatter and laugh and dandle children and crack their lobster-claws. Tables scrape and bang, and the waiters banter as they bustle to and fro, adding to the din that echoes off the vaulted roof. The place might not catch the eye of a Michelin inspector, or appeal to those who seek luxury: but you will not eat better fish in Spain, nor, as far as I know, in Europe. The swordfish steaks, when they arrive, are as tender as veal, and the curved pink-and-white carapaces of the king prawns evoke the arches in the mosque at Cordoba.

Outside El Puerto de Santa Maria there are various beaches, although the nearest is dominated by harbour cranes and tower blocks. Further out, back towards Rota, is the more agreeable resort of Vistahermosa, with scattered estates of Florida-style villas and a fine setting on a great semicircular bay. Nearby is a

Left The church of Santa Maria de Milagros, Puerto de Santa Maria. Above the plateresque south doorway the Virgin stands upon a tower, symbolizing her role in the Christians' capture of the castle nearby.

Above The rolling plains of Cadiz province, with some of the lushest pastures in Andalusia.

recently developed marina complex, Puerto Sherry, with a hotel, villas, and a full array of sporting and shopping facilities.

In the other direction, 20 kilometres to the south-west, shining white across the bay like a clipper ship under full sail, is one of the oldest cities in Europe. Cadiz was founded around 1100 BC by Phoenician traders and has been continuously occupied ever since, by Carthaginians, Romans, Visigoths and Moors. The security of its inner harbour and its convenience as an entry-point to the Iberian peninsula have resulted in a number of apogees in its long history. According to Pliny, Cadiz was the only surviving fragment of Atlantis, which was submerged beneath the sea in the same cataclysm that dried up the Sahara. Subsequently it became one of the chief markets of the Mediterranean: for the cattle of Hercules's tenth labour (the hero is depicted on the city's coat of arms), for the gold and silver of the Tartessians, for Cornish tin and Baltic amber in the seventh century BC, for Roman saltfish and dancing girls (the forerunners of today's flamenco dancers), and for Inca gold. This was the second largest city of the Roman empire, Gades Jocosae, a louche and free-wheeling resort and a religious centre sacred to Melkarth, Hercules and Aphrodite. Later it replaced Seville as the sole inlet for the wealth of the New World. Between times it was harried by Viking raiders, by Barbary corsairs and by the English under Drake, who singed the King of Spain's beard here in 1587, and Essex, who sacked the town in 1596. At other periods it was too insignificant even to be worth sacking — when it was captured from the Moors by Alfonso the Wise in 1262 he found it almost depopulated, and by the end of the eighteenth century it was described by an English visitor as shabby and 'insufferably stinking'.

Cadiz no longer stinks — it is one of the cleanest seaports in Andalusia — but thanks to the attentions of Essex few of the surviving buildings predate the seventeenth century. On the long causeway that leads to the town the architecture is strictly modern, an agglomeration of tower-blocks and factories; but at the far end an imposing mid eighteenth-century gateway marks the entrance to the original settlement. Continu-

ing round the left side of the peninsula, you soon pass the two cathedrals on your right. Of the old cathedral little remains except a massive tower: it was begun in the thirteenth century, but was burnt by Essex, who, unlike Drake on his more famous raid, put his men ashore and occupied the town for two weeks. The new cathedral, dating from the eighteenth and nineteenth centuries, has attracted much critical abuse. The English traveller Joseph Townsend called it 'a disgrace to taste' in 1787 — when he can only have seen a part of it — and Ford compared it to 'a stranded wreck on a quicksand'. (Haydn, however, was inspired to write his *Seven Last Words from the Cross*.) Certainly its long period of construction is reflected in its appearance. Despite its dramatic situation beside the sea (the pounding waves can be heard in the crypt during a storm), it baffles the eye with the mismatched colours of its elements, superimposed on one another like some dubious ice-cream confection: chocolate base, vanilla towers and statuary, and orange dome.

The interior, with its massive pillars, round arches and dominant dome, is more coherent than the exterior, and there are some early eighteenth-century stalls from the Charterhouse at Seville. A museum contains a number of gigantic gold and silver custodials, the biggest some 6 metres high, and various generally indifferent sixteenth- and seventeenth-century paintings by Zurbarán, Ribera, Morales, Fernandez and Murillo, none of which matches those in the Fine Arts Museum (see below).

Cadiz is a pedestrian's city. Crammed into its narrow peninsula, like a finger pointing out to sea, it is a tiny Moorish Manhattan, certainly like no other Spanish city. The streets run arrow-straight, with glimpses of sky or trees at the ends. Underfoot they are cobbled, and the buildings on either side, looming taller than their actual height because of the constricted space, are enriched with jutting Arab windows and wrought-iron grilles. Wedged into these alleyways are a number of churches.

The most interesting are in the Calle de San

Lanterns on the Atlantic shore, Cadiz.

Francisco, the furthest of the long streets which run north-west up the peninsula. San Agustin has a 1647 façade and contains a Christ by Andalusia's leading sculptor, Montañés, and a 1666 reredos, in which the Virgin is set within a small round boudoir – a *camarín*. Santa Cueva (at no. 11) has a round eighteenth-century oratory containing frescoes, three of which (1793–5) are by Goya. They are among his few religious paintings, and the *Last Supper*, said to be based on a drawing by Poussin, unusually shows the group recumbent, as though they were celebrating the Passover. At the end of the street the church of San Francisco, with a detached belfry sprouting from the adjoining houses, overlooks a pleasant square. The church was restored in the early seventeenth century, but contains some attractive Moorish-style stucco-work, especially in the flower-filled cloister.

Zig-zagging a block left and north you reach another square, the Plaza de Mina, much larger and greener, a leafy refuge in this idiosyncratic but claustrophobic city. At one corner stands the Fine Arts Museum, where an eclectic little collection spans four or five centuries and includes north European as well as Spanish art. The pick of the paintings is a large group of twenty saints by Zurbarán, which were brought from the Charterhouse in Jerez, and there is also a fine *Ecce Homo* by Morales, which outshines the same subject by Murillo, a tiny canvas by Rubens, only 30 centimetres tall, and work by Van der Weyden. On the ground floor is the Archaeological Museum, containing relics from the city's Phoenician heyday in about 500 BC, notably a sarcophagus and the capital of a pillar. There are also Roman sculptures, including a headless woman who for some centuries was worshipped as the Virgin.

Half-a-dozen blocks south-west of the plaza is the Oratorio of San Felipe Neri (1679–1719), with a Murillo over the altar. While King Ferdinand VII was a prisoner of the French, Spain's first liberal constitution was proclaimed here in 1812, a document much admired in the rest of Europe, but short-lived. Not long afterwards Ferdinand returned to the throne but failed to keep his promise to uphold the new democratic constitution and was captured by the revolutionaries. He appealed for help to his former enemies, the French, who had failed to capture Cadiz in the Peninsular War, and a force under the Duke of Angoulême marched to his rescue; the fledgling democracy had its neck wrung. Next door is the Historical Museum, which contains a fine mahogany-and-ivory model of the city in the eighteenth century. Note how every house had a patio and a well, in which rain-water was collected: Cadiz has no water of its own, and only survived the French siege in 1811–12 with the help of shipments from Puerto de Santa Maria.

From here you can walk back south-east to the cathedral, discovering in the process – especially if it is a warm day – that Cadiz is rather larger than you thought. The other sights of the city are best admired by driving around the perimeter. At the south-west corner, you can walk out seawards through a gate in the old town wall, the Puerta de la Caleta, which leads to a fort built in 1613, possibly on Phoenician foundations. The view from here takes in a small curve of palm-lined beach with a miniature castle at each end and fishing-boats drawn up on the shore. Past the left-hand castle, the Castillo de Santa Catalina, is a lush stretch of park with another fort at the far end, the Candelaria, behind which is an equally lush baroque church. This is Nuestra Senora del Carmen, Our Lady of the Garden: it contains the grave of Admiral Gravina, the Spanish commander at Cape Trafalgar, where the combined Franco-Spanish fleet under Villeneuve was defeated by the British under Nelson in 1805. The Cape itself lies only 40 kilometres to the south; Villeneuve sailed out from Cadiz, and its citizens could hear the cannon-fire of the battle.

Cadiz' other chief attraction – apart from the fish-stalls down by the harbour – is the wealth of its festivals. The pre-Lent Carnival in February has been declared of international interest, and features a fancy-dress parade in which crowds of revellers accompany the floats, and teams of troubadours roam the streets with drums and horns, singing satirical verses. On the

---

Cadiz: in the words of Byron, the 'Siren of the Ocean'.

final Sunday papier-mâché dummies filled with toys are hung from trees and lamp-posts and broken open at midnight. Later, in Holy Week, there are more processions (as there are throughout Andalusia) and others again in spring and summer.

When you are ready to leave Cadiz, drive south along the peninsula. The road turns inland before the Isla Leon at the southern end, whence Hercules stole the cattle of Geryon, and runs past the factories and salt-pans of San Fernando to Chiclana, known for its white wines (*pastos*). From here the highway continues down to Gibraltar; but if you have time you can detour to the east to visit Medina Sidonia, once the home of the commander of another, greater Spanish fleet, the Invincible Armada.

Medina Sidonia rises high above rolling fields of wheat and sugar-beet: long before you reach it, the church crowning the town flashes white in the sky. Sidonia refers to the Phoenician town of Sidon, while Medina signifies the Moorish town founded here 1200 years ago. Some of the Arab fortifications still remain, and the town is entered through a much-photographed double-horseshoe gateway, the Arco de la Pastora, at the top of a steep cobbled square planted with orange trees.

Narrow streets lead to a long lozenge-shaped square, with a neat renaissance town hall at one end, and a bar where you can gather your strength for an assault on the town's summit. The way is steep, leading up out of the square through an arch, and emerging onto a small yard in front of the fifteenth-century church of Santa Maria. There is a strange, desolate, almost haunted feeling up here. The church walls are peeling and splashed with lichen, gold against the bright blue sky, and a few metres away, standing alone among the wild-flowers that cover the bare hillside, is the squat tower where Blanche of Bourbon was murdered at the behest of her husband Pedro the Cruel (see p. 20). Pedro's aunt Leonor de Guzmán – the commander of the Armada two centuries later was also a Guzmán – sheltered here too, and she too was put to death.

The inside of the church is very pleasing – a wonderfully simple gothic structure, marred only where splashes of whitewash have turned the vaulting

skewbald. The great reredos, dating from 1575, is one of the finest you will see, a mellow old-gold assembly of sculptures in high relief.

The scant relics of the rest of the castle – apart from Pedro's bloodstained tower – are on the hilltop above, a short walk away. There is little to see, except for Andalusia spread out around you. Driving back down to the bottom of the village, and out on the road south to Vejer and Tarifa, you are launched into some of the richest countryside in this part of Spain. There are no hedges to obscure the sweep of wheatfields and meadows, with the hills ranged behind. By summer's end this is all bleached and bare, but in May there are flowers in ribbons along the road, and in great splashes on the hillsides . . . dark red vetch and scabious, lupins and big pink poppies, and the all-pervasive purple bugloss. Fighting bulls graze here and there, like the beasts that enliven medieval tapestries, and white egrets flap and peck wherever any moisture still lingers.

Vejer de la Frontera towers above the intersection with the main coastal road, its fortified acropolis a reminder that – as the town's name confirms – this was for many years a war zone. After its final capture from the Moors, Vejer became, like Medina Sidonia, the property of the Guzmán family, who covered the herby hillsides around with beehives.

It is a congested little place. The cobbled alleys wind around themselves, and if you try driving you will soon find yourself confronted with an impassable archway or a flight of steps. The views in every direction are stupendous – Africa is clearly visible to the south and the mountains of Ronda to the east – but they can only be glimpsed through gaps between the old houses. Huddled together at the top of the town are the restored remains of a small castle (now privately occupied), together with the handsomely mouldering arches of a monastery, above which agitated swifts dodge the circling kestrels. There is also an austere little church with a rose window over the very plain west door, traces of painting on its south wall and blue

Medina Sidonia, seat of the commander of the Armada.

Above The fifteenth-century church of Santa Maria Coronada, Medina Sidonia. Inside, a spectacular reredos depicts scenes from the life of Christ.

Right Medina Sidonia. The name commemorates the Phoenician town of Sidon.

Left **These slopes below Vejer de la Frontera were once covered with bee-hives.**

Above **Vejer de la Frontera, where a fighting bull is run through the streets on Easter Sunday.**

tiles on its battered tower. The golden stone of all these monumental relics contrasts handsomely with the whitewashed houses around them. In April they have the Fiesta del Toro here, when the bulls run loose in the streets.

Ahead of you as you descend from Vejer is another vast stretch of the Costa de la Luz (see p. 37) . . . flat, featureless and largely uncommercialized. This is an entirely different coastline from the Costa del Sol, east of Gibraltar, and the Costa Blanca, round the corner in eastern Spain. It lacks the backdrop of mountains, and is generally short of sporting and eating facilities: but it also lacks the high-rise blocks and the intensive farming which have ruined the Costa del Sol. And the sand is far better – white and purged by the Atlantic instead of gritty brown and littered with plastic detritus.

For the anti-social and the mildly adventurous, the Costa de la Luz is, apart from short stretches elsewhere, the best in the south. Accommodation is often scant and many of the coastal villages are, well, scruffy, but at least they are undeveloped. Moreover, this coastal region claims an exotic and varied cuisine, even if many of the delicacies are easier to find in the tourist brochures than on any restaurant menu. Special sea-food dishes include sardines with peppers, tuna with tomatoes (this is an active tuna-fishing area), bream with onions, *chocos* (a local squid) with beans, ray in paprika, swordfish and flying-fish in saffron sauce, *urta* (an indigenous white fish) in cognac, dogfish in marinade, shrimps in batter.

The closest of the local beach resorts, if you can call them that, is Conil de la Frontera (that militant suffix again), which lies down a side-road a few kilometres back towards Cadiz from Vejer. Its sole historic relic is a square tower, the keep of the former castle, daubed around its merlons with red paint, as though with smears of lipstick from some long-forgotten revel. Beyond is a stupendous beach of bright sand, so wide that the sea is barely visible at low tide. On both sides the bay curves serenely round, to Cape Trafalgar on the left and Cape Roche on the right. But a 'no parking' sign and a dearth of facilities augment a feeling of inhospitality, and you would do better to work your

way through the fringe of the town to the north to the Playa de Fontanilla. Here you can drive down onto the beach and park beside an agreeable restaurant, which specializes in sea-food and serves the *pasto* of Chiclana, a pale sherry-type wine. The beach is narrower than that to the south, and hence more apt to fill up in summer, but also more picturesque, backed by high dunes that shade to red cliffs as they climb towards the lighthouse at Cape Roche. Far out to sea, lines of pink fishing floats flicker on the water like browsing flamingoes.

There are hotels at Fuente del Gallo and El Roqueo, a little further north, and here and there the villas and low-rise apartments are beginning to sprout from the fields of mustard and the thickets of umbrella pines. Come back here in a few years' time and you will find – for better or for worse – that it is much changed. A new housing development is burgeoning at Roche, a short detour off the main road north, but there is still a steep walk down to the narrow, pretty beach and the accommodation is currently only in chalets and tents. The beach extends to Barrosa, reached by road from Chiclana, opposite which is the lighthouse of Sancti Petri, built on the site of a Temple of Hercules.

If, instead of doubling back this way, you head south from Conil, you find yourself bumping along a dirt track which follows the long, empty beach. The flat landscape is enlivened only by the occasional Moorish watch-tower and eucalyptus grove, until the road climbs through pleasant pine-woods to cross Cape Trafalgar, and the little port of Barbate appears below. Behind it the hills rise to the Sierra de la Plata, and the coastline runs on down to Gibraltar. There is a sardine fair here on the beach in August. Ten kilometres further on is Zahara de los Atunes, named after its tunny-fishing. The amateur can fish for tunny with a line; the professionals herd the great fish inshore into a maze of nets and club them to death, until the sea runs red.

Zahara is a physically humble little place, with few buildings rising above two storeys, and outside the tunny season it is more than half asleep. It has the remains of town walls, some bars and restaurants, a huge beach, and an atmosphere which you may

The Costa de la Luz has the longest, cleanest and emptiest beaches in southern Spain.

interpret as charm or squalor, depending on the weather and your state of mind. The inlet behind it, which gives it the feeling of an island, is full of egrets, and before the water-meadows dry up in summer they are patrolled by skeins of peasants searching for snails.

From here a road runs back up on to the main highway, where you can again turn south. Away from the shore you are back amid the great rolling meadows, the grazing-ground of fighting bulls, and on several occasions the battlefield of men. Back near Chiclana the French were defeated in the Peninsular War by a combined force of 4000 British and 13,000 Spanish (although the British later complained that 'no stroke was struck by a Spanish sabre that day'). Earlier, in 1340, Alfonso XI defeated Yusuf I of Granada and his Moroccan ally Abul Hassan, the 'black sultan' of Fez, despite the use of cannon by the Moors, for perhaps the first time in European warfare. And earlier still, on almost the same ground, a small encounter took place

which was a forerunner of one of the more influential battles of European history: Tarik the invading Berber had his first brush here with the huge army of Roderic the Goth, prior to shattering it a few kilometres further north on the banks of the Guadalete.

Today, as in Flanders, the spring flowers have appropriated the battlefields. As you drive south, the flatlands which were once marshes are now lakes of bugloss, and the hillsides shine with a roseate glow which proves, on closer inspection, to be the blossom of that dour Gaelic weed, the thistle. Nor are flowers the only pleasure. If you have time to leave your car and walk or picnic, field-glasses at the ready, you will see that the skies are the patrolling-ground for a variety of raptors: short-toed and booted eagles, griffon and Egyptian vultures, harriers and kites and buzzards. Easier to spot are the storks. If you have not already seen them nesting on church-towers, look out for a colony in a small oak-wood beside the road east of Vejer. There are shrikes too, and the brilliantly-coloured rollers and bee-eaters. Down here at the bottom of Europe the land is singed with the flames of Africa, which conjure up a number of its birds, and its animals too: out in the scrub, if you wander far enough, you may see a mongoose or a genet, or the quick-footed green dragon, the ocellated lizard, which grows to a metre long and eats rabbits.

Fifteen kilometres short of Tarifa you can turn off to the right to Bolonia, to visit the remains of the Roman tunny-fishing port of Bella, or Belo. The road climbs a ridge before winding down to the most perfect little bay in southern Spain. The Romans, like monks, knew where to build. The curved shore, with a rocky headland at each end, is of blinding white sand and the sea is a crystal green. Behind you are the flowers and ahead is Africa. There is a small huddle of houses and clutch of beach bars. The ruins themselves are scant, and if you are expecting Baalbek you can save yourself the detour. Down by the shore, barely visible among the weeds, are the stone tanks of the fish-factory where the tunny were salted, a reminder of the times when Cadiz enjoyed a monopoly of the salt-fish trade. Before the days of refrigerators, salt-fish was a valuable commodity, and still exists in the form of *bacalao*, the salted and dried cod of Spain and Portugal, as stiff as a board, and pungently detectable at a distance of several paces.

Uphill are the remains of the little town, with a forum lined with shops, a bath-house, a platform for the temples of Juno, Jupiter and Minerva, and a few worn front-stall seats in the theatre (the size of which suggests that the town was, after all, not so little). Today few stones stand upon one another, and the loudest sound is that of the onshore breeze among the thistles.

Ahead, as you continue towards Tarifa, a huge rock is visible down the coast. Gibraltar at last, you think: but you are looking at the other Pillar of Hercules, Jebel Musa, in Morocco. You are now approaching the southernmost tip of Iberia, with Africa only a few sea-miles away across the clashing waters of the Atlantic and Mediterranean. The clash creates a region of gales: the magnificent beaches on this final stretch are given over to wind-surfing. To the ornithologists the air above the Strait, however turbulent, has another significance. It is one of the two major routes to Africa for millions of migrating birds (the other is across the Bosporus). In spring and autumn, when the thermals are right, the great raptors lumber into the telescope lenses of the watchers at Tarifa or Gibraltar, struggling to gain height, mobbed by hostile gulls. Unlike the lighter warblers and swallows they often have a hard time of it, and fly low overhead, low enough to reveal the desperate glint of their eyes.

Tarifa is one of that handful of European towns whose walls are virtually complete. They were taken from the Moors in 1292, as is attested by an ivy-mantled plaque beside the horseshoe-arched entrance; and two years later they were the scene of one of Spain's military legends. The Moors, bent on recapturing the town, sent an ultimatum to the Christian commander, Alonso Perez de Guzmán: unless he surrendered, they would kill his son, whom they had in their power and exhibited before the gate. Kill him, said Guzmán, and threw down a dagger. For this heartbreaking loyalty the Spanish king conferred on him the town of Sanlucar and the land west of the Guadalquivir, including the Coto Doñana: and as we have seen, the family later became the dukes of Medina Sidonia.

Through the west gate, the Puerta de Jerez, the late gothic church of San Mateo soon appears on the left. It has a pleasing west front, although the white sculptures and baroque doorway clash rather disconcertingly with the grey stone of the façade. The interior is disappointing, with clumsy vaulting. Towards the sea is the castle, which dates from 960. It is now (or, should I say, still) a military base and is closed to visitors, but you can climb up onto a walkway which circles the Moorish town-walls. At one point a belvedere offers a view over the Strait to the huge rocky mass of Jebel Musa, and there are glimpses down into the town and vistas of the coast, until the walkway is interrupted by the breach made by the French in 1811, when Tarifa again successfully resisted a siege. Inside, at ground level, there are pleasant cafés and restaurants among the humble shabby houses, together with that indefinable atmosphere which you get inside a small walled town – the sweetness of the kernel inside the nutshell.

Driving eastwards over the Cabrito Pass, where the Sierra de Ojen rolls down to the Strait, you at last have a view of Gibraltar ahead: while to the south, across what seems to be a narrow lake, there is the occasional glimpse of a round-topped mountain, which contrasts weirdly with the lush foreground. It is Jebel Musa again, and at sunset it turns red: through binoculars it is wrinkled with purple shadows, hard and dry, older-looking than the rocks of Petra.

Gibraltar lies on the far side of Algeciras Bay, not quite opposite its twin Pillar of Hercules on the African shore. Both are named after the protagonists of the Moorish invasion: Jebel Musa after Musa Ibn Nusayr, the Tunisian Eisenhower who master-minded it, and Gilbraltar (Jebel Tarik) after the general who led it — not to be confused with Tarif, who commanded an earlier reconnaissance expedition and gave his name to

Tarifa, the southernmost corner of Europe. Near here the Moorish invaders first set foot in Spain.

Tarifa. Tarik was the one who (if you believe a French chronicler quoted by Ford) developed his own way of living off the land: he killed his prisoners and served them up to his soldiers.

As for Algeciras itself, the best way to appreciate it is to ask a companion to read its history to you while you drive past without stopping. During its capture by the Christians in 1344, iron cannon-balls were used for the first time in European warfare, and the Knight in Chaucer's *Canterbury Tales* numbered this famous siege among his campaigns. But nothing now remains of its walls or other former glories.

Our route now leaves the coast, following the C3331 to the north, shortly before the turn-off to Gibraltar. The road runs through cork-trees, with their strange two-tone trunks: a dark chocolate-brown at the bottom where the bark has been harvested, and the normal puckered grey at the top. In 10 kilometres another turning to the left leads to Castellar de la Frontera. This narrow but perfectly adequate road climbs through a wilderness of oaks and rocks, inhabited by wolves and bears. Unless you too are of nocturnal habit you will not see them: a more likely sight will be Egyptian vultures, or other examples of the raptors which are common hereabouts.

Suddenly a castle appears ahead, high on a rocky knoll. As you approach it through pink cistus and oleander the forest dies away, the view widens and a lake opens up below. There are a few houses scattered outside the beetling entrance fortifications, which you must enter on foot. Students of military architecture can pause here to admire the three successive archways which an assailant must penetrate, while ornithologists can sit with their backs against the warm stone and watch the several pairs of kestrels which nest in the masonry.

Inside, a surprise awaits. This place is not so much a castle as a tiny Moorish town. Or rather a ghost town. Until recently Castellar was a refuge of hippies, but the Spanish government ejected them in order to restore the principal buildings. Apart from the fortifications

Africa lies beyond this horizon.

Alleyways on a mountain-top: the fortified village of Castellar de la Frontera.

there are only two, a small church and an equally minuscule town hall. The rest of the space enclosed by the walls is filled by a labyrinth of low hovels, penetrated by plunging alleyways which occasionally offer glimpses of the splendours of the surrounding countryside. Remote, claustrophobic, a little spooky, Castellar imbues you with the sense that little has changed here since the Moors were ejected back in the fourteenth century.

Returning to the C3331, continue north to Jimena de la Frontera, where another castle stands on a hilltop above the village. Like Castellar, it is Moorish (recaptured in 1431), with another triple gateway: but this entrance section of the wall — a few metres of worn stone in which Roman tombstones are visible beside the door — is almost all that remains, apart from the round keep at the highest point. You can wander around the bare hilltop tracing the course of the curtain walls and the outlines of the buildings within,

81

and picturing the scene in times of siege, when the inhabitants of the village below would take refuge in here, and fill every available open space with their flocks and camp-fires. At the lower end of the bailey, next to a modern cemetery, you can see the underground cisterns and storage chambers, massively vaulted, and all around is a wild panorama of mountains and rocks and cork-forests, with Africa, the homeland of the men who built this castle, visible to the south for the last time.

Driving on north, look back on Jimena and see the blades of rock jutting up around the hilltop like dragon's teeth, which made it such a natural site to fortify. But keep an eye on your road too, since it is now a corniche which hugs a ridge above the boulder-strewn bed of the Hozgarganta river far below. All traces of cultivation have disappeared, and you are afloat on a sea of blue hills, the western end of the national park of Cortes de la Frontera. After 30 kilometres you reach a pass, and 15 kilometres later turn off the Jerez road towards Algar. By now the scenery has changed again. The mountains have withdrawn, and in the spring the road is bordered by waist-high grass and meadows of purple bugloss, punctuated with the gnarled black trunks of solitary cork-oaks. Cross another ridge, and the bugloss has given way to yellow hillsides of Spanish broom, and then to rolling fields of wheat and sugar-beet and olives. At last, atop a great cliff on the far side of a river, the skyline ahead is filled with the roofs and towers of Arcos de la Frontera.

Arcos is my own favourite among all the small towns of Andalusia. As dramatically sited as Ronda (see p. 87), but without the encroaching suburbs and the influx of tourists from the Costa del Sol, it has a uniquely balanced charm. It is both quintessentially a hilltown and quintessentially Andalusian. Compressed along its narrow ridge, with steep cliffs on either side, it is a self-contained little world of cobbled alleys and archways, of whitewash and golden stone, of tiny patios and huge churches. For a short stay, Arcos is perfection. It even has one of the best of all the paradors.

On the way in you can stop to visit the eighteenth-century convent of La Caridad, a short detour to the right immediately after crossing the River Guadalete. It has a dainty, almost frivolous white façade picked out with baroque details in dark-red brick, and a pretty patio inside. Continuing up into the town centre, the road soon passes through the eastern gate, the Puerta de Metrera, where you may be disconcerted to see the Virgin peering down at you through the glass of a renaissance window, like a proprietorial châtelaine. Both she and the window contrast strangely with the stern Moorish merlons of the wall above, which serve as a reminder that Arcos was described by Alfonso XI as 'the strongest town of our realm'. Previously it was the Roman Arcobriga, and before that an ancient Iberian settlement. But the streets that you are passing through now are largely Moorish, and make no concessions to the motor-car. The next few minutes will be as hair-raising a drive as any corniche in the sierras. Keep your nerve and follow the signs, and after various vicissitudes and changes of level and direction you will arrive at a square at the top of the town, on one side of which lies the parador.

It is a modern building, but you would not know it at first glance, since its non-committal whitewashed façade blends well with the rest of the square. What makes it memorable is its situation. To appreciate this you must pass through to the terrace at the back and walk to the railing on the far side. You are on the edge, the very edge, of a sheer, 100-metre cliff. Far below, seemingly close enough to toss a rose into it, the Guadalete loops in an almost complete circle, enclosing a miniature amphitheatre. To the right of you rises a tower of the castle. To the left the church of San Pedro rears its bulk against the sky: it is far along the ridge, yet in this clear mountain air you can hear the creaking of the ropes when its bells sound the hour. And below you, especially at dusk, is perhaps the most remarkable sight of all. Nesting in the sandstone cliff are several pairs of kestrels, which emulate the dozens of swifts around them, swooping and gliding and sharply turning. The jackdaws do likewise, and even the rock-doves fold their wings and plunge like peregrines. As the light fades the tempo of these graceful antics increases, until the air is filled with hurtling projectiles, intoxicating, unforgettable.

Opposite the parador is the town hall, and behind that is the castle, almost hidden from sight. To one side of the parador, the square is open to the outer world, and here you have a similar view to that from the parador's terrace. The fourth side of the square is filled with the sandstone wall of the church of Santa Maria. This has long maintained (and still does) a rivalry with San Pedro further along the ridge, and once sent a deputation to Rome to establish which church had priority in Arcos. It was 44 years before the answer returned. Santa Maria had won.

The southern view of the church is dominated by the handsome square-topped tower, dating from the 1750s. Its truncated appearance is due to the fact that it was never finished, or, if you believe the local guides, that it was trimmed by the earthquake of 1755. The west façade is a sumptuous example of the Isabelline gothic style (or, as a local brochure disconcertingly translates it, Elizabethan gothic), but admiring its lush convolutions is difficult – it towers high above a narrow street at the head of a flight of steps, with no room to stand back.

The interior is sombre, cluttered, but full of riches, including one of the finest sets of baroque choir-stalls in Andalusia. These are carved from five kinds of wood and are two-tiered, with plaster-encrusted balconies that curve over them like breaking waves of icing-sugar. The church also contains a curiosity, which is in fact a kind of anachronism: a wall-painting that dates from the end of the fourteenth century, although the main structure of the church is sixteenth-century. Hence the painting must be a survival from the earlier Visigothic church on this site. It has been described as the most important Italo-gothic painting in the south, but the style is more romanesque, even byzantine, with golden halos glowing out of a background of faded blues and greens and pinks, and a totem-pole of saints on either side rising to grimacing stone lion-heads at the top.

In a chapel on the right is a painting from the school of Murillo which is of interest only for what Alfonso Lowe says about it in his admirable guide to the region (1973). It was, he says, hung over a hole in the wall which contained the church treasures at the time of the French invasion in the Peninsular War. The painting was of so poor a quality that it escaped the eye of that acquisitive patron of the arts, Marshal Soult, and the treasures survived.

For the avid doorway-collector, there is a fair example a couple of hundred metres down the street in the narrow façade of the palace of the Count of Aguila, dating from the fifteenth century. The frontage has been highly praised, but it is modest enough, with a small plain doorway flanked by pilasters as slender as needles. All the interest is in the detailing. Animals and grotesque heads lurk in the friezes. Heroic figures top the pilasters, and above the door, set in its Arab frame, is a Moorish double-window which has blossomed into pure gothic.

From here you can walk anywhere – Arcos is a walker's town and every alleyway is a delight – but most of the other buildings of interest lie towards the east. Passing Santa Maria again by a road that threads between the north wall and a buttress, you almost immediately pass another doorway on the left, that of the convent of the Incarnation. Like the west front of Santa Maria, this is Isabelline gothic, with a double-bend arch topping the sadly weather-worn doorway. On down Paradise Street and around the corner is the seventeenth-century convent of the Mercedarias Descalzas, the barefoot ladies of charity. Although full of architectural delights, it is closed to visitors. Opposite is the market, its truncated entrance-pillars testifying to a former grandeur, but now characterized only by a huddle of bustling stalls and a smell of fish.

Either of the streets above or below the market leads to the other great church, San Pedro. This is older than its rival Santa Maria, having been fashioned out of the fourteenth-century Moorish fortifications. But its age is not immediately apparent from outside, since the façade and tower are four hundred years later. They are all of a piece, a simple creation of yellow stone, weathered in places to a grey that accentuates the high-relief of the detailing – Corinthian columns, sundry urns and figures, and a balcony topped by a small broken pediment. In the middle sits St Peter himself, in his papal hat.

Inside, the gothic vaulting is simple but unremarkable, the eighteenth-century choir-stalls are inferior to those of Santa Maria, and the reredos of 1547 is handsome but gloomy – the paintings within its fine old-gold framework are almost invisible. In a side chapel on the left are a pair of banners captured from the Moors on the banks of the Guadalete in 1484, and elsewhere are two of the many surviving mummified bodies of St Victor and St Fructuoso.

There are two palaces next to San Pedro, the Casa de los Virues and, round the corner to the west, the Palacio del Mayornazgo, with the gothic chapel of La Misericordia opposite: and if you came here along Nuñez de Prado Street you will have seen others. To east and north there are more, hidden in a maze of alleys. The lesser sights are largely those of an Andalusian village, but enhanced by the extra wealth of this proud little town, and by the narrowness of its eagle's-nest eminence, with sudden views outwards on either side. Antique pillars prop up the street-corners, and open doorways reveal delightful patios: any one may contain old arcading, or a well-head or mounting block, and all will be rich in pots and flowers and songbirds.

The streets themselves are almost as rewarding as the buildings ... rising or falling, turning to yield a stretch of whitewashed wall to the sun, or to reveal a

Arcos de la Frontera, traditionally founded by a grandson of Noah.

renaissance gateway. Beneath your feet the cobbles suddenly give way to flights of steps, and overhead, against a cobalt sky crowded with hurtling swifts, arches support the towering walls and unify the whole. In Holy Week these streets are thronged with spectacular celebrations. Ancient floats have been specially designed for threading the narrow alleys, and on Easter Sunday they run bulls through the town.

Before leaving Arcos you may want to sample the wine. Although carrying the town's name, it is made from grapes grown at a lower altitude – the winters up here are too chill. The white wine is fresh and agreeable, but the red is flabby, belying its claim to have been aged in oak. It may seem odd that red wine grown so far south cannot match the robustness of its counterparts in southern France or Italy, but this is a white-wine soil.

From Arcos you can drive back west to Jerez, or north to Seville, or east by a stunningly beautiful road to Ronda. Whichever your destination, take the time to drive around the ridge on which Arcos is built, and look up at it. On the north side you pass the end of an artificial lake. From the south the full scope of the castle is visible, as it is not from within the town. From either direction the serried buildings, floodlit by the sun, stand out magnificently against the sky. Some hilltowns – the pueblos of Arizona or the strongholds of Tuscany – seem to grow from the hills they crown, and merge with the rock. But not Arcos. From the crest of the great cliff its white walls, golden castle and belfries shine in the air like a challenge: the battle-cry, for many centuries, of one faith against another.

ANDALUSIA

Sierra de las
Harinas

Teba

*Embalse de
Guadalhorce*

Sierra de Lijar

Olvera

Torre Alhaquime

*Embalse
del Chorro*

Algodonales

Cabañas

El Chorro

Setenil

Ardales

Cuevas del
Becerro

Zahara de los
Membrillos

El Burgo

*Puerto
del Viento*

Grazalema

Guadalhorce

Montejaque

Ronda

Serranía de Ronda

Benaojan

Parauta

Cartajima

Alpandeire

Cortes de la Frontera

Juzcar

Farajan

Sierra Bermeja

El Colmenar

Genal

Marbella

Gaucin

Costa del Sol

Gibraltar

0   10   20 km

N

3
The Mountains of Ronda

Ronda – Teba – Setenil – Olvera – Zahara de los Membrillos –
Grazalema – Cueva de la Pileta – Ronda la Vieja – the Genal valley

The ruggedness of these mountains makes men strong and agile, and warlike,
because it was always on these frontiers that the wars were waged against the
Christians. These people teach their children when young how to shoot with the
crossbow, and through their zeal in this art they are masters, who would never
fail wherever and whenever they shoot.

Hernando del Pulgar

In the fractured landscape of Andalusia, where every town has its own character and its own history, Ronda can match them all for romance and individualism. Hidden in the heart of the most vertiginous mountains of the south, impregnable behind its famous cliffs, the town was long a refuge for brigands, smugglers and warriors, a law to itself. (Richard Ford, an ambivalent hispanophile, said that the smuggling in these parts was the only well-organized system in Spain.) Settled by the Romans on a far older site, Ronda became a semi-independent kingdom under the Moors and a defiant outpost against the advancing Christians until the last years of the Reconquest. Since then Ronda has been famous for knife-play, horse-breeding, bull-fighting and – for over a century – tourism.

To appreciate the full drama of its situation you should seek out a view of the town from a distance. On the C341 from Gibraltar and Gaucin there is a side-turning to the west, less than a kilometre from the entrance to the old town. It is marked only by a small cluster of houses and is unpaved. You will know you are on the right track if you find yourself following the crest of a ridge, with a Moorish watch-tower to the left, and on the right an unfolding panorama of Ronda. It lies along the top of its cliff like a row of glinting teeth on an immense gaunt jaw-bone. Moreover this jaw is fractured in the middle, from top to bottom, by a fissure through which, by a cataclysmic freak of nature, the Guadalevin flows between the two halves of the town, the newer Christian sector to the left and the Moorish on the right. Immediately you can see how impregnable Ronda once was.

There is more to see if you complete the couple of kilometres to the end of the ridge. Keep right along the crest to a vivid grove of umbrella-pines where you can park the car. The view is now not merely of Ronda and the lush valley below it, but of a huge expanse of scrub and oak-woods to the left, backed by the encircling mountains. Ahead of you, on the very tip of the ridge, is a house which was occupied for a while in the 1950s by the painter David Bomberg, who produced a series of views of Ronda in bold scarlets and oranges and whites, piling the pigment onto the canvas with a verve that matches the subject.

Just before you reach the house, down a side-track to the right, is a curiosity of a different kind: one of Andalusia's few Mozarabic churches, i.e. churches built by Christians during the Moorish occupation.

Moreover this example belongs in a smaller class still, being one of a handful of troglodytic Mozarabic churches, that is, carved out of the solid rock. Although the Moors tolerated the continuation of the Christian religion, there were evidently instances – as here, in this cliff at the far end of an isolated ridge – when the Christians felt obliged to worship discreetly.

What you will see as you approach this church of La Virgen de la Cabeza is a newer, eighteenth-century extension standing outside on a shelf of rock. The original chapel is dug into the hillside on your left. Beside the entrance is the kitchen, with a fireplace and recesses to hold water-jars. The main part of the chapel is a crudely carved cave, interrupted by modern supports of brick, with a round-topped altar recess at each end, and a burial vault with shelves for three significant corpses, perhaps bishops. At the west end are more rock chambers – the residential quarters. Everything is rough and neglected (though this may change, since the church is now under restoration), and it takes a wrench of the imagination to picture the tiny Christian community gathered here in the tenth century, heads down, waiting for the storm of Islam to pass by.

Back on the main road, you can make another detour immediately outside the walls of Ronda, where a road leads down to the left. After a kilometre or so this brings you to the river, where there are traces of Moorish water-mills. These are hard to find among the figs and poplars, and you would do better to look up. A little way upstream to the right is the Puente Nuevo, the eighteenth-century bridge that spans the great gulf, the *tajo*, which divides the town. The 100-metre piers are stupefying: massively square, they rise the full height of the gorge from the narrow river-bed to the sky. They carry three arches, above the centre of which is the tiny neo-classical window of the former jail. To the left and right, and directly above you, the cliffs rise sheer. With the sun full on them, they are as smooth as if worked with a plasterer's trowel. Along the topmost rim tiny figures lean over railings and look

down on you. It is like a view from a plane, inverted.

Drive back up to where you left the main road. It was here that Ferdinand of Aragon arrived by a secret march in 1485 while the town's commander, the redoubtable Hamet el Zegri, was away on an expedition. Even with the advantage of surprise Ferdinand might never have captured Ronda – the Christians had tried often enough before – had it not been for his new weapon, his siege artillery. In the preceding days his great bombards had smashed down the walls of the Moorish strongholds outside Malaga, and here at Ronda he switched from stone to metal cannon-balls. Despite the desperate attempts of El Zegri to raise the siege, the town was compelled to surrender. The old hornets' nest was smoked out at last, and the whole western sector of the last Moorish kingdom subdued.

The walls in front of you (largely reconstructed) are dominated by the Almocabar gate, which is Moorish, with a double archway between two rounded towers. To the left of it is a later, sixteenth-century entrance, and high on the right, its gold bulk dominating the scene, is the church of the Espiritu Santo, the oldest purely Christian church in Ronda. This was begun in 1486 to mark the point in the walls where the Christian cannon created the first breach. The interior is agreeably economic – a single whitewashed room beneath gothic vaulting.

Beyond the gate is the old Moorish town, small enough to stroll around in an hour or two. Turn left in a couple of hundred metres and you will find yourself in a square dominated by the sixteenth-century church of Santa Maria. It was, as usual, adapted by the Christians from the former mosque, and the brick tower is massively Muslim below and ornately Catholic above. The church's façade is covered by an attractive and unusual addition – a colonnaded loggia of three storeys. It must have provided an excellent view of the bull-fights which were held in this square before the construction of the famous ring on the other side of the *tajo*.

The most interesting part of the interior is the recently uncovered *mihrab* of the mosque: a tiny recess with carved Arabic inscriptions. The main structure of the church reflects a transitional period of architecture

The valley of the Guadalevin, below Ronda.

Left The great gorge, or *tajo*, which divides the old Moorish quarter of Ronda from the new town.

Above Cobbles in the sun: the old Moorish quarter of Ronda.

and a chaotically slow reconstruction: the west end is gothic, but east of the choir the style is renaissance, with high vaults in pale stone, lit by tiny clerestory windows.

The square outside was formerly used not merely for bull-fights, but also as the parade-ground of the castle, which stood at the far end opposite the church. It was blown up by the retreating French in 1809 and finally demolished by the monks of the Sacred Heart to build their present college. The square also contains the eighteenth-century town hall, the convent of Clarisas and the church of La Caridad. From here you can stroll around the two sectors of the old town which lie on either side of the through road.

Turning north-east first, walk down the street to the right of Santa Maria, and cross the main road. Opposite you is an almost perfect little fourteenth-century minaret, apart from its Christian bonnet. It has a narrow Moorish doorway and austere window-slits, but no accompanying mosque: this has disappeared, and the tower juts incongruously from a house. A little way northwards, where the street turns and descends, the palace of the Marqués de Salvatierra appears on the right. It was rebuilt in 1786 after a fire, but retains an early seventeenth-century façade in a late renaissance style. This features two pairs of figures which are said to have come from Mexico. If so, the Mexicans here show a unisexual – but only partial – sense of modesty: on the left only the man hides his genitals, on the right only the woman.

Continuing below the Salvatierra palace you find yourself outside the town, on the edge of the *tajo*. Above are the ancient walls. Below, an eighteenth-century arch leads to two bridges, the so-called Roman bridge on the left and the Arab to the right, although the former is mostly Arab and the latter mostly Christian. Beyond them is the newer half of the town. You can climb through it, back up to the main road, but there is little to see, and it will be much quicker to retrace your steps.

But first pay a visit to the Moorish baths, which date from the thirteenth or fourteenth centuries and are largely intact. They are sited on the floor of the valley to the right of the bridges, and were fed by an aqueduct that ran along the top of the wall between them and the river. An open patio with brick colonnading like a cloister leads into the interior rooms, where horseshoe arches support barrel-vaulted roofs, pierced with the traditional star-shaped holes that illuminate the crypt-like gloom. These main rooms, warmed by the hot-air ducts beneath the floor, were for resting and hobnobbing after the bath; off them are subsidiary chambers that contained the plunge-baths and the furnace.

Climbing back up the hill, keep right at the Salvatierra palace, and you will soon see on the right the House of the Moorish King, named after a celebrated palace built on this site in 1042. The present twentieth-century building is hardly worth visiting. Permission can be gained from the owner, who sits in a small antique shop further up the street, but she tells a sad tale of recent vandalizations which have stripped house and garden bare. The site is still dramatic. The garden is perched on the rim of the *tajo*, and from it descends an underground flight of steps (now unlit and not negotiable) which were famous throughout Andalusia during the Moorish occupation. There are over 250 of them, and it was up this dark and slippery hell-hole that the Christian slaves carried the water which supplied the town.

At the top of this street, just before the main road, the convent of Santo Domingo stands on the right. Gothic in style and dating from the early sixteenth century, it was once the headquarters of the Inquisition. Much of it, especially the cloisters, has been in a ruinous state for years, but recent restoration gives some indication of its former elegance, with lofty vaulting, a gallery, and a fine coffered roof.

Beyond is the entrance to the Puente Nuevo, Ronda's most famous piece of architecture. Completed in 1788, it replaced the two lower bridges above the Moorish baths. Leaning over the parapet you can look straight down on the narrow trickle of the Guadalevin

---

The Salvatierra palace in Ronda. The figures and wrought-iron balcony are said to have been brought here from Mexico.

Old stonework in Ronda. Some of the palaces are built on Roman foundations.

far below and hear its distant splashing. From further still, out in the valley, the clucking of hens is borne up on the clear mountain air, and the sky is filled with the antics of martins, doves and kestrels. The cliffs of the old town fall sheer on either side. One precipice is crossed by an ancient irrigation channel, furrowed out halfway down, on a face so smooth that you shudder to contemplate the construction of it. Opposite, below the rim of the new town, are terraces with restaurants where you can sit and view the drama of the scene.

Returning to the old Moorish sector, turn right off the main road down Tenorio Street. On the corner is a restaurant which, on my last visit, served *tapas* of dried pulses which neatly symbolized two major aspects of Andalusia's history: the chick-peas had originated in the Middle East, the corn kernels in America. Many of the houses in this street have a handsome local feature – ground-floor windows that project on pedestals, like oriels. You emerge into a little

park set on the cliff-edge, with views down into the valley. Turn left at the far end, and you are soon standing outside one of the finest of the palaces whose massive entrances punctuate the whitewashed streets. This is the Mondragon Palace, a former royal residence under both Moors and Christians. The simple renaissance doorway is flanked by pairs of classical columns and topped by a balcony set in an early baroque frame. No Moorish influences here. The rest of the stone façade is sternly defensive, except for a pair of renaissance loggias at the upper corners. The little entrance hall has a carved roof and a mounting-block, and to the right are the old stables, with a massively beamed ceiling and brick arcading that once held the mangers. Inside the palace are two sixteenth-century patios. From the first of these a stairway beneath a painted dome leads up to a salon that boasts a fine 500-year-old coffered roof decorated with golden suns.

There is another fine interior in the Giant's House, a short distance away behind the church of Santa Maria. Its name is derived from a badly-worn Roman figure set high in the exterior wall. Although much restored, this is the only surviving Moorish palace in Ronda. It dates from the fourteenth century, and contains a central patio with columns which are a hundred years older, horseshoe arches, some surviving Moorish plasterwork, and an *artesonado* roof.

Apart from a few traces of Roman masonry, little is now visible from Ronda's pre-Moorish period. But in the basement of a house opposite the Mondragon Palace archaeologists recently found relics from the Bronze Age, and beneath them traces from the Copper Age, and lower still from the neolithic period: proof that the town has been continuously occupied for 6000 years – far longer than the vaunted 3000 years of Cadiz. Today, such things must be felt rather than seen. In the words of the poet Rilke, a long-time resident and the fashionable 'discoverer' of Ronda at the turn of the nineteenth century, it is 'a little city without any objects worthy of mention, unless it be the object of her whole existence . . . her place in the pattern of all that is most heroic'.

There is, however, an object worthy of mention on the far side of the Puente Nuevo – the famous bull-ring. Built in 1785, it is the biggest and most beautiful in the country, and the oldest, except for a square one in northern Spain. The symmetry is superb. Uniquely, it has two stories of colonnades covering the seats, surmounted by a tile roof. The masonry, the round O of sand within it, all is the colour of gold. Seldom has a place of death been so handsome. The manner in which the death took place is also significant: here in Ronda, the year after the ring was completed, the whole style of bullfighting changed. Hitherto it had been an aristocratic sport, and the bull was fought on horseback, as at Jerez. But the king withdrew his favour, and the nobles did likewise: so a Ronda *torero*, Pedro Romero, transformed bullfighting into a people's sport. As the people had no horses, they met the bull on foot. Romero thereby saved bullfighting, and with it the breed of fighting bulls. On the other hand he killed 6000 of them, the last at the age of eighty. His genius was reincarnated a century later by another Ronda bullfighter, Cayetano Ordonez, a friend of Ernest Hemingway, who was a frequent visitor here. Today, the town still celebrates its bullfighting traditions during its September celebrations, the Goyesca festival, when the *toreros* wear early nineteenth-century dress and women parade the streets in local costume.

Leave Ronda by the Seville road, but turn off it to the right while still in the northern suburbs, following signs to Malaga and forking right again onto the C344. A short way out of town are the remains of an aqueduct, which has the mass of a Roman creation but the horseshoe arches of a much later date. After a few more kilometres you are winding over the Pass of the Winds. This, you feel, would not be a good place to break down. The landscape is scrubbed clean by the gales, bare of vegetation, multi-coloured in pink and grey, and utterly empty. Huge boulders litter the hillsides as though discarded by a feckless Creator. The ground lurches down to the left, and sweeps away to an immense mountain vista beyond. Then the road itself plunges into a steep and narrow cleft, with great rough cliffs on either side. It is with something like the relief that medieval travellers must have felt that you spy ahead the village of El Burgo.

Heat and dust: summer temperatures regularly top 37°C in the bare valleys east of Ronda.

Its original inhabitants found a sharp-edged knoll on which to build, so that despite its site in a valley, the village has the compactness of a hilltown, and traces of its Moorish fortifications are still visible. Inside, you find yourself in a typical, unfrequented, working Andalusian village. This has advantages and disadvantages. The streets are plain rather than pretty. You walk on cement, not cobbles. But around you are the black-clad women and the laden mules which are gradually disappearing from southern Spain. And if, as I did, you forget to pay at the bar, nobody will chase you for your money: it was ten minutes before we remembered and turned back, filled with embarrassment. '*De nada*' said the young girl behind the counter: 'Don't worry about it.'

From El Burgo you can cut through north-east to Ardales, if the road is open: otherwise you can head north to pick up the C341, and make the loop east and south. Ardales has caves and traces of a castle, but you

ANDALUSIA

may as well bypass it on the MA444 and drive on towards El Chorro. Before you reach this village there is a turning on the right which leads to the monolithic church of Bobastro and to a viewpoint over the River Guadalhorce, but you can safely bypass this too: the church ruins are much less impressive than those outside Ronda, and the rest of the settlement does not warrant the scramble up the hillside.

At El Chorro, a bridge over the Guadalhorce leads to the railway station, where there is a bar and restaurant with a swimming-pool, and the start of a path back along the river. You are now in a narrow gorge with beetling cliffs, and you have in fact already passed the most famous sight a kilometre back: La Garganta del Chorro, the Throat. This is a cleft, only a couple of metres wide, where the river slides between 100-metre precipices. The railway is dramatically engineered along the cliff-face, and more horrific still is a footpath which inches along the sheer smooth rock, and crosses the Throat on a hanging bridge as insubstantial as a spider's web. It begins back at the station, and runs through the cleft to the lake beyond.

Retrace your route past Ardales and drive north. Almost immediately the road emerges from the rocks and pines, into a rolling plain of sunflowers and wheat and barley. Behind you are the red-and-white hills that hide the gorge, and on your right is a wide lake. Its rambling inlets and soft banks look natural, but it was created by damming the Guadalhorce. Ahead rises the stumpy castle of Teba. To reach it, turn right when you hit the C341, and then detour to the left, crossing the battlefield where the Scottish warrior the Black Douglas, with the heart of his king Robert Bruce in a silver casket round his neck, met his death in 1330. He was actually en route for the Holy Land, to bury Bruce's heart in holy ground, but stopped at Seville to get some early practice against the infidel.

You can drive most of the way up to the castle, but the last few metres must be climbed on foot. There is little to see except a bare bailey across the pate of the hill, marked by perimeter towers. The most picturesque remains are an octagonal tower, grey with golden corner-stones and a high keyhole arch, and the keep at the highest point, with barrel-vaulted rooms

and carved insignia over the usual first-floor entrance. It is now garrisoned by sheep, who have found their own entry, and peer from the tattered windows like outlandish sentries. Nearby is an underground cistern or dungeon, and the breezy walk around the rim reveals the inevitable views. The village below is shabby and appears to have been sited in an ash-tray, beneath a hill without a blade of grass. As you peer down, spare a thought for Douglas, fighting the good fight in full armour and high summer, on a plain where the temperature can hit 40°C.

Return to the C341 and head back towards Ronda. The cornfields continue to extend to the right, but on the left the mountains close in. Beneath them the unrolling rural tapestry displays a series of panels: meadows give way to olives, and then to a river-course lined with poplars and eucalyptus. Everywhere there is a great peaceful emptiness. Farmhouses are few, and over 20 kilometres elapse before the road passes a village. This is Cuevas del Becerro, a walled stronghold on a cliff above the river, where the route turns right on to the MA414.

The little road meanders up an enchanted valley, rich enough to sustain small herds of cows and sheep. These are rare in Andalusia. More common are the huge droves of goats, black and grey and chestnut, with their lonely goatherds, relics of a bygone pastoral existence that recalls the parables of the Bible. After a dozen kilometres, turn off to Setenil, an architectural curiosity which is, in its way, unique.

The village lies along the banks of the Trejo. When you reach the river, turn right following signs to the *cuevas*. At once you see why the place is famous. Many of the houses here are built underneath an overhanging cliff: peer through the entrance of a bar, and you will see that the rear wall and roof are of solid rock. When claustrophobia begins to impinge, drive back to the main road and up to the top of the village, past a solitary watch-tower and a church of yellow stone which contrasts with the white houses. The street

Autumn ploughland in the remote expanses west of Teba.

96

Above The plain near Teba, where the Scottish warrior, the Black Douglas, with Robert the Bruce's heart in a casket round his neck, lost his life in battle against the Moors.

Right The upper part of Setenil is typical of many villages in Andalusia, but the lower town is unique: here, houses are built under overhanging rock along the River Trejo.

Scratching a living from the wilderness: olives and fragmented ploughland west of Teba.

narrows to a needle's eye, but soon debouches into a little square, high up but dominated by an even higher cliff. Here you can park and explore the scant castle ruins, or seek out the fine coffered roof in the town hall, or walk along under the cliff to a flight of steps which leads down into the lower town.

Leave Setenil through the arch at the top of the square, and drive on through a softly rural landscape of cornfields and eucalyptus thickets, fringed as always by mountains behind. After a few kilometres you pass on the left the fortified village of Torre-Alhaquime, and then, breasting a ridge, you are confronted by one of the most dramatic townscapes of all. Whereas Arcos and Ronda were stretched like tiaras along their cliffs, Olvera has a silhouette like a viking helmet – a dome of white houses on a hill, from which the twin peaks of church and castle thrust like horns.

'Kill your man and flee to Olvera' was once a common saying, at a time when this place, tucked far away from coast or city or river, was a den of thieves and a refuge for cut-throats. Later a poet wrote more admiringly: 'Olvera may consist of a street, a church and a castle – but what a street, what a church, and what a castle!' Today all three look modest. The main street still flows serenely down the hill: for a couple of hours each day its fine houses throw a strip of shadow down one side or the other, and you will see that spectacle characteristic of hot countries – the entire male population standing in line, gossiping or idling, hugging the narrow shade. The church, alas, is tediously neo-classical: but the castle, though tiny, is worth a climb, and you can solicit the key from a house below the acropolis.

The small tree-planted bailey conveys a feeling that the whole fortification has been contrived in miniature. The round-cornered keep is unrestored – a rare blessing in these parts – and along the cliff-edge, like sentries, stand little pepper-pot towers, barely big enough to hold a man, each with a perfect vaulted roof under its pointed hat.

Below the wall of the keep, next to the modern steps that lead up to the first-floor entrance, is an unusual feature: a barrel-vaulted water-cistern with a chimney at one end which leads up inside the keep, enabling the occupants to lower buckets for water without the need to go outside. The keep itself has three vaulted storeys, with a spiral staircase leading to the roof. Make the climb, if you have the lungs and the time. The view from the top is breathtaking, even by the standards of a land of spectacular views. The spreading mantle of brown roofs below, compact, many-angled, tilting away into the sun, typify all the reasons that make Olvera such a satisfying place to visit. Beyond them is a lush arena of sloping cornfields and tumbling olive plantations: and all round these farms are mountain ranges as tumultuous as their names – Conejos, Lijár, Harinas, Zarzapardal, Zaframagon.

As you leave Olvera on the N342, heading west, there are even finer views of the town than on the approach road. Near the Puerto Cabañas pass, it appears for the last time, high in the sky, above a landscape of earth and trees, flowers and crops that

Torre Alhaquime, a fortified hill-village south of Olvera.

seems to embody every shape and colour. Beyond the pass, you can see what gave Olvera its former remoteness: the road funnels into a hostile wilderness of rock and scrub. At Algodonales, 22 kilometres further on, turn south on to the C339 heading for Ronda.

Almost at once, at the site of a new dam and reservoir, is the right-hand turning to our next destination: another in the archipelago of white villages that rise, castle-crowned, from the sea of green and brown. This islet – Zahara de los Membrillos, Zahara of the Quinces – is one of the steepest. Its steepness has ensured its place in military legend. The town was considered so impregnable that an unattainable woman was nicknamed a *Zaharena*: but it was

stormed by the Moors in a surprise night attack in 1482, at a time when it was a Christian outpost on the frontier, and thereby lit the fuse that fired the last campaign of the Reconquest, culminating in the capture of Granada. The next year it was recaptured in an equally athletic assault, commemorated by the castle and ladder which appear in the village's coat of arms.

The approach road winds up past a sixteenth-century watch-tower and into a narrow square. There is a small hotel here, for those wishing to spend a night or two in this remote eyrie, and at the far end stands the church of Santa Maria. It was built by one of the Figueroa family, founders of the local baroque style which culminated in the churrigueresque. Its chief decoration, however, is provided by nature: an elaborate rock-garden of flowering plants decks the lintel of the north door and continues up the roof to the very pinnacle of the short spire with its herringbone pattern of blue and white tiles. The church is set right up against a cliff. High above, there is a glimpse of the castle keep, round-cornered like the one at Olvera. This is one climb that is barely worth the twenty minutes required, since little of the castle survives. On my last visit, however, there was a bonus: a pair of golden eagles circling low around the hilltop.

There are colourful celebrations here on the feast of Corpus Christi, when the village is decorated with branches: and there are more processions and fireworks at a *fiesta* in August, as there are at Olvera, and at our next port of call, Grazalema. The last can be reached direct from Zahara, or by making a 10-kilometre detour west off the Ronda road, towards Arcos. This diversion is worthwhile: there is something special about Grazalema.

Part of the village's distinction is due to its site. It lies close beneath the highest and bleakest of the inland mountain ranges, the Sierra de Grazalema, which gave the treasure-galleons returning from America their first glimpse of Spain – despite being 80

kilometres inland. From the crest (a climb I would not recommend to a casual visitor), two glints of snow are sometimes visible in the distance: to the south, the Atlas Mountains in Morocco, and to the east the Sierra Nevada, both some 200 kilometres away.

The cobbled streets of Grazalema are broader and straighter than in other villages, the tiled roofs wider, and the black-painted window-grilles bigger, their hard lines against the whitewashed walls reminiscent of a half-timbered medieval town. Small though it is, Grazalema is demurely gracious and dignified. In mid July the demureness slips a little, when bulls are run through the streets in a miniature version of the more famous celebrations at Pamplona in northern Spain.

There are two churches here, one eighteenth-century and another – the more interesting – in an earlier gothic style. There are also bars, restaurants and a hotel. Grazalema's charm has brought the tourists, and farmhouses can be rented nearby. But though the village has lost its virginity, it is still visually unsullied. As in all Andalusian villages, the shops are invisible behind the sheets or bead-curtains that mask their anonymous doorways. This makes shopping tricky, but strolling down the flower-decked mini-boulevards is a delight. At the bottom of the village is a little square, where my wife and I refreshed ourselves with sharp black coffee and velvety brandy, after negotiating the murderous pass that crowns the road from Arcos. This is not the place to extol the virtues of Spanish brandy, especially on an empty stomach, but as we lolled in the blinding sunshine, beside a strange fountain with four flat stone faces like African masks, we remembered how Laurie Lee described a similar visit to a similar place: 'We sat by the roadside, drinking wine and screwing up our eyes.'

The C344 back to the Ronda road leads through rocky scrub punctuated by oak-trees and, in April and May, drifts of four types of *Cistus*: the white *C. × corbariensis*, white, maroon-blotched *C. ladaniferus*, mauve *C. albidus*, and bright cerise *C. crispus*. The terrain opens out into lush meadows where pigs graze: this is another region famous for its Sierra-cured hams. Ahead the valley is bounded by escarpments as sheer and regular as battlements, and far away to

Foothills of the Sierra de Lijar, west of Olvera, for centuries a refuge for outlaws.

the right is the bleak massif of the Serrania de Ronda. Three kilometres to the south after regaining the main road there is a right-hand turning to the Cueva de la Pileta, with its palaeolithic and neolithic rock-paintings.

The paintings are much less impressive than those at Altamira in northern Spain (though some are older), or at Les Eyzies in the Dordogne: but the scenery on the 13-kilometre drive from the highway is as dramatic as any in Andalusia. The road, small and rough but perfectly adequate, is dominated by the bare crags on either side, with vertical strata that snarl like dragons' fangs. Between these massive outcrops, in peaceful contrast, are little strips of meadow and the glimpse of a lake. The road used to be the smugglers' route between Ronda and the coast, and still makes a splendid through-drive via Cortes and El Colmenar. It burrows ever deeper into the narrow valley, until Montejaque appears ahead, splashed on the hillside. After the next village, Benaojan, the cave is signposted to the right.

If there are cars in the small parking-space, you will know there is a tour in progress. Scramble on along the rough stone steps that round the shoulder of the cliff, and in 50 metres you will reach the entrance to the cave. If there are no cars and the cave is closed, sound the car horn vigorously and perch on a rock looking down into the valley. A figure will emerge from a white farmhouse and walk up to you. The Cueva de la Pileta is privately owned, by a farmer whose grandfather first discovered the cave in 1905, when searching for bat-manure.

Inside there are caverns of varying sizes – the tallest is 12 metres high – where stalactites droop overhead and stalagmites stand like dimly-lit statues, multi-coloured from the stains of different salts. Where the walkway has been excavated, the rock tells the story of the site's human habitation: chipping away the surface has revealed successive layers of black and white,

Grazalema, said to be the wettest village in Spain. In July, after the fiesta of the Virgen del Carmen, a bull is loosed through the streets.

indicating soot that was subsequently covered by limestone precipitated from the water which flows through the cave in wet weather. There are twelve such pairings of black and white. During twelve local ice ages, men came into this cave for shelter. Perhaps they also came for religious ceremonies, since some of the paintings are thought to be fertility symbols. The discoverers of the caves found other relics too – skeletons and fragments of pottery – but these have been removed to museums elsewhere.

The inner sector, where the paintings survive, is guarded by an entry cleft less than a metre wide, through which a stream of bats pours past the visitor's head like Homer's squeaking spirits of the dead. The paintings, executed in a blend of animal fat and iron oxide, are mostly small, seldom exceeding postcard size. The oldest, from the palaeolithic period some 25,000 years ago, are the more interesting: executed in shades of red and black and yellow, they show a pregnant mare, goats, an enormous fish. The neolithic drawings, in black monochrome, are confined to arrowheads, a bow, and several obscure scratchings (perhaps calendars) like primitive games of noughts-and-crosses. Artistry has declined with time.

Before returning to Ronda, another detour can be made. As with the Cueva de la Pileta, you may find the journey more rewarding than the end-objective. Soon after returning to the main road, take a left turn to Ronda la Vieja. It is about a dozen kilometres away, through scenery quite different from that of the valley on the way to the cave. This road winds upwards through what almost resembles English parkland, with meadows and wide-spaced oaks. You can picnic very agreeably on a ridge among the broom and cistus, with fine views both ways, and shade to keep the wine chilled.

Old Ronda, when you reach it, is open all day, and a resident guide will admit you, free. Its name is misleading. This was the Roman settlement of Acinipo, a contemporary neighbour of Arunda – Ronda itself – and far bigger, as a stroll around the site soon reveals. Built over an earlier Iberian and then Phoenician town, it was finally destroyed by the Vandals, and nothing now remains except forlorn piles of stone widely

Left Lush pockets of cultivation alternate with jagged mountains on the way to the Cueva de la Pileta, near Ronda.

Above Outcrops of the Serrania de Ronda near Montejaque, on the old smugglers' trail to the Mediterranean.

scattered across the hillside among the yellow mustard-flowers, and the grotesquely restored stage of the great theatre. But the site is superb. You are 1000 metres up, and from the top seats in the theatre there is a 360° view, with Setenil and Olvera clearly visible, and the Serrania de Ronda looming to the south. No other houses stand anywhere near, and there is no sound except the wind, the cicadas and the sheep-bells. As you stroll around, in the stillness and utter desolation, you gradually appreciate the size of the circuit – at least a kilometre across – where the massive walls ran. The town once had a vast amphitheatre, as well as the theatre. Now it is an abandoned mason's yard, with its stones long gone to build towns and villages throughout the region.

Return to the main road, and within a few kilometres you are back in Ronda. If time permits, there is another circuit you can make to the south, lasting two or three hours. Head towards Gaucin and Gibraltar, on the C341. This is one of the old Royal Roads, once used for herding cattle, with verges 50 metres wide where the livestock could graze as they were ushered along. Since pesticides have been scarce in these parts, such roads have become a haven for wild-flowers, and here in the mountains you will find the yellow-and-brown *Fritillaria hispanica* in the ditches in April, the stately clear-blue *Scilla lilio-hyacinthus* in the wood-edges, and the dark-blue tufts of *Muscari plumosus* in the young corn: also the lilac blue *Iris sisyrinchium*, the pink garlic, *Allium roseum*, and the deep blue *Anchusa*, together with the spotted cerise butterfly orchid and at least two others, the buttercup yellow *Oprys lutea* and the reddish-brown *O. tenthredinifera*.

After a dozen kilometres a side-road, the MA515, leads off to the left. It clings to the rim of the Genal valley and links a string of villages which are as characteristically Moorish as any in Spain. Unlike more exposed areas, the population of this secret enclave largely escaped eviction after the Reconquest, so that although Arabic has not been spoken here since the seventeenth century, the physiognomy of people and architecture must be very much what it was in Moorish times. And the scenery is consistently breath-taking. As well as the flowers below and the towering rocks above, there are great chestnut plantations that change in autumn to a blaze of gold: while, for the botanically inclined, a tree found nowhere else in Europe grows on the limestone slopes further east. This is the *Abies pinsapo*, a fir with short needles and cinnamon-brown young shoots.

After about 8 kilometres the first village, Alpandeire, suddenly appears below, with steep streets, a large church, and a tang of mule droppings. Then comes the less pretty Farajan, followed by the tiny Juzcar, set amid chestnut groves. From there the road climbs past Cartajima to the last and best of the five villages, Parauta. This lies isolated at the end of a 3-kilometre diversion, set against the mountain, and its houses are architecturally distinctive — taller than normal, and tapering from bottom to top.

This medieval, tortuous, enchanting meander lasts for only a couple of dozen kilometres, but the lush saucer of the deep valley below is almost like another country, green and fertile, with red earth and tumbling streams, humid, seemingly dumped here at random among the bleakness of the surrounding mountains. The circuit ends at an intersection with the C339. To the left is Ronda. To the right lie the golden flesh-pots of the Costa del Sol, and another world.

The country west of Ronda is one of the most inaccessible corners of Andalusia. Part of it is a national park, home of the wild goat, *capra hispanica*.

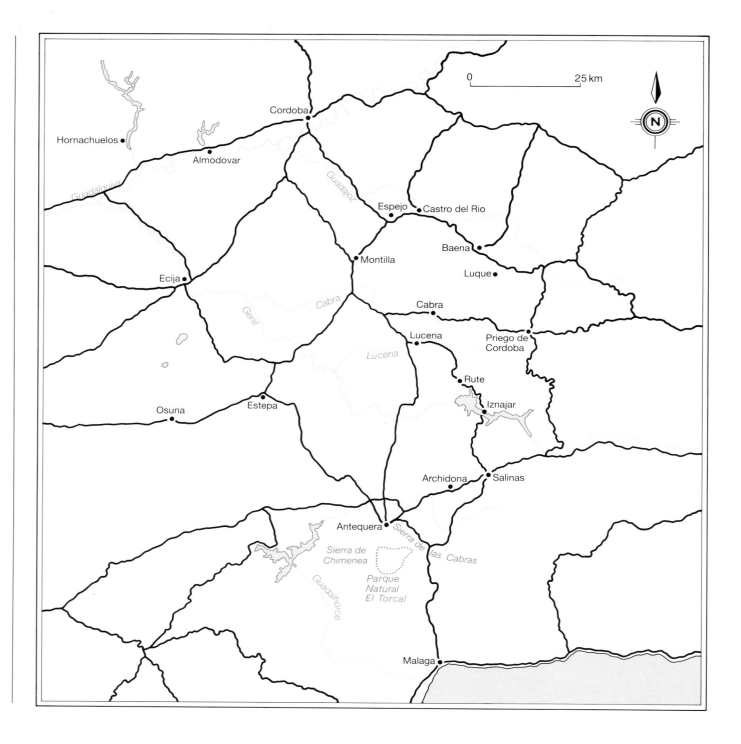

4
Cordoba and Central Andalusia

Cordoba – Medina Azahara – Almodovar – Ecija – Osuna –
Estepa – Antequera – Archidona – Lucena – Cabra –
Priego de Cordoba – Baena – Castro del Rio – Espejo

. . . A cloud of dust, left in the air when a great people went galloping down the highroad of history.

José Ortega y Gasset

Few of the world's great buildings have an exterior as deceptive as that of the mosque at Cordoba. At first glance it resembles a vast, dilapidated, antediluvian warehouse: or perhaps, to judge from the projecting buttresses and merlon-topped walls, a long-abandoned castle. Then you become aware of the decoration – some brightly restored, some sun-bleached and worn – where the bare dusty wall blossoms into brief displays of pink-and-white keyhole arches, pierced-stone windows, blind arcading, glints of marble and flurries of plasterwork. These are the only hints that within lies something very important, very Muslim and very old.

This secrecy derives from the Muslim mentality. Most Muslim buildings, religious or domestic, have blank and humble exteriors, and many have entrances with dog-legged passages, so that the luxuriance of the patio within is only seen after the second turning. Hence the words of the popular ditty:

Mine is the same condition
As the house of the Moorish king:
Outside the plaster is rotting
But treasure lies hidden within.

The mosque at Cordoba is also characterized by its age. It was begun in the eighth century, more than half a millennium before the Ottomans developed the more familiar mosque architecture of huge domes and slender minarets. These later clusters of minarets are largely decorative (only one is required to call the faithful to prayer), whereas the minarets in Spain and North Africa are thick and square and functional.

Apart from its history, the Cordoba mosque offers a chance to study the layout of a complete building of this kind, and how it derives from various precepts of the Islamic religion. The *mihrab* indicates the direction of Mecca, the pilgrim's goal, and the whole building is oriented on this axis, so that the worshippers can face the holy city while they pray. (Islamic bedrooms and privies are deliberately oriented differently, to avoid inadvertent sacrilege.)

The second point to note is that a mosque is not narrow like a Christian church, but broad, because prayer is believed to be more efficacious when proffered from the worshippers at the front (who are nearest to Mecca). Hence there is a desire to fit as many people into the front row as possible. Thirdly, the faith requires the entire population of adult males to worship together on a Friday, so that a mosque must be able to accommodate them. And fourthly, ritual cleansing is an essential preliminary to Muslim worship. Amongst the dozens of orange-trees here in the Cordoba orangery – possibly the oldest walled garden in the world – are the fountains which in their original form served for the ablutions of the faithful (provided they had been reasonably chaste – carnal intercourse required a complete bath). One of the feeder-pipes of a baroque fountain has subsequently acquired another function: a spinster drinking from it will become married within the year. The courtyard also accommodated any worshippers who could not fit inside the mosque: this end of the building, now separated from the orangery by a wall, was originally open, and the orange-trees (or, in Moorish times, more probably palm-trees) continued the rows of the columns inside.

Now, however, the mosque is entered through a doorway which is aligned with the original main entrance to the orangery under the refurbished minaret, the Penitents' Gate, and with the *mihrab* at the far end of the mosque – the Mecca axis. What this mode of entry loses in authenticity it gains in drama. The change in light is sudden, and for a moment you pause on the threshold. Then, as your eyes adjust to the gloom, you become gradually aware of standing on the fringe of a sacred grove, a forest of stone columns . . . or perhaps of a vast crypt, since the darkness seems subterranean. In front of you and on either side is row upon row of pillars, linked by double arches, one upon the other, in white stonework that alternates with pink brick. The overall effect is both uniform, with the basic elements repeated and repeated in endless perspectives that render the mind giddy, yet also diverse, since the details vary. The 850 columns, some from San Vicente, the church that previously stood on this site, others collected from ancient ruins as far afield as Carthage and Istanbul, are of many styles, ages and materials – Roman, Visigothic, Byzantine and Moorish, of marble, jasper, breccia, porphyry and granite.

The scale is immense. Somewhere in here is an entire Christian cathedral, yet as you set out timidly down one of the long aisles it is nowhere to be seen. This first part of the mosque is the original section, begun by Abderrahman I in 785. At its far end, where the floor rises slightly and the exterior of the cathedral appears on the left, the original *mihrab* has disappeared, but slightly beyond it is the site of the second *mihrab*, built by Abderrahman II when he extended the mosque in the ninth century. It was redeveloped by the Christians in 1371 as the chapel of Villaviciosa, in an elaborately decorated mudejar style. Behind the chapel are two more, and ahead is the third addition to the mosque, built by Al Hakam II in the tenth century.

Here the columns are more ordered, with uniform Corinthian capitals and with the colours of the marble alternating regularly. A section of the ceiling is illuminated, showing the fine detailing between the carved beams, and as you near the far end the double arches suddenly explode into a cross-over design, with chased plasterwork between the component stones. This change in style introduces Hakam's great *mihrab*. It is preceded by the Caliph's private enclosure, behind which the entrance arch is set in a frame of lush byzantine mosaics, gold and blue and green, purple and red. The surrounding tracery resembles the later plasterwork of Seville and Granada, but is here carved from white marble. Dating from 965, this *mihrab* has been described as one of the crowning achievements of Moorish art. Alternatively it might strike you as being, dare I say it, in indifferent taste, a polychrome extravaganza with a top-heavy construction, where the delicate detailing of the mosaics and plasterwork is weighed down by the height and bulk of the arches and vaults. It is in any case poorly lit – even with the aid of a coin-operated light – and as a final irony is aimed not at Mecca but at darkest Africa.

To the left is the last extension of the mosque, by the great warrior Almansor in 990. This deprived the *mihrab* of its central position, but was essential for the accommodation of a larger congregation, at a time when Cordoba was at the height of its power. With its

The orangery of the mosque at Cordoba. The rows of trees – originally date-palms – echo the lines of pillars inside the mosque.

Above The characteristic double arches in the mosque at Cordoba were a device to give extra height to the low columns.

Right The mosque at Cordoba: the roof of the antechamber to the *mihrab*, built by Al Hakam II in the tenth century.

Six kinds of marble in the mosque at Cordoba.

3000 mosques, 300 baths and 28 suburbs, the city had grown to eclipse all others in the Muslim world except Baghdad itself.

Almansor – 'the Victorious' – conquered every Christian capital in Iberia, but he was less impressive as an architect. His addition to the mosque (recognizable by its brick floor and by the vaulted roof added in the eighteenth century) matches the rest, but the capitals of the columns are simpler, and the arches are not what they seem – the red-and-white effect is painted on, not built-in. Unlike Granada, where the Moorish craftsmanship progresses over time, here it regresses.

The Christian cathedral was inserted in the first half of the sixteenth century. The gothic vaulting in the sanctuary and transepts is elegant enough, and there are very fine choir-stalls, carved in 1758 from Cuban mahogany. But much of the decoration would seem florid anywhere, let along amidst the magnificent simplicity of the mosque. It is like a sudden flourish of brass-band music inserted into a clavichord sonata.

If you return outside the mosque and face Mecca – or, in this case, Chad – the next building on the right is the episcopal palace. Part of the surviving structure dates from the fifteenth century, but long before that the site held the palace of the Roman and Visigothic governors, and the original *alcázar* of the Caliphs, who connected it to the mosque with a bridge. The right-hand street from the far end of the palace leads to the 'new' Christian *alcázar*, begun in the late thirteenth century by Alfonso X ('the Wise'), though the current structure dates from 1328. It is small, but the gardens at least are worth the short detour.

These are not as extensive as the *alcázar* gardens in Seville, nor as authentically Moorish as those in Granada, but they are still amongst the finest in Andalusia. They are on the site of the original gardens, which were watered by the great wheel (now restored) in the nearby tower on the banks of the Guadalquivir. The creaking used to keep Queen Isabella awake when she stayed in the *alcázar*. (Alexandre Dumas, describing a similar water-wheel in 1846, said it made a sound like a man having his throat cut.)

The upper gardens were part of Alfonso's layout. Of the many former fountains here, only two square ponds survive, and these were enclosed with iron fences in the seventeenth century, after the poet Góngora's sister pushed the bishop's page into one of them. Around them are shady walks and parterres filled with plumbago, bougainvillea, aloes, lilies, palms, bananas and trumpet vines, and stretching away below are the newer gardens, with their shining pools and leaping jets of water.

Apart from Isabella and Ferdinand at the end of the fifteenth century, the castle's most noted subsequent inhabitants were the Inquisition, who made it their headquarters until 1821. Inside the entrance is a suitably severe patio, dominated by the castle walls, beyond which a series of passageways leads to the vaulted Hall of the Mosaics. The mosaics, mostly in geometric black-and-white, are hung on the walls and are less impressive than those at Italica (see p. 32). In a nearby room are some other Roman relics, notably a third-century sarcophagus in such immaculate con-

Horse-drawn landaus offer an indulgent way to tour Cordoba.

dition that it looks brand new. The high-relief sculpture shows pairs of figures beside a half-open door, so that the soul could stroll out into the Underworld. There are barley-sugar columns at the corners — forerunners of those so common in baroque architecture.

Beneath these rooms are baths, currently unrestored and less interesting than others to be seen elsewhere. Above, a walkway along the ramparts leads to two of the four corner towers, one of which contains a chapel. From the top of the taller can be seen the city, the river, and the great bridge. Built on Roman piers, though much restored since, it is a reminder that under the Emperor Augustus Cordoba was capital of Spain, as it was later under the Caliphs. At the far end is a fortified tower, La Calahorra, Arab in origin and refortified by the half-brother of Pedro the Cruel after Pedro had besieged the city. It is now a museum, where the displays include relics of the poet Góngora, whose sister misbehaved beside the garden pool.

Emerging from the *alcázar*, walk straight ahead across the gardens, where Christians were allegedly martyred under the Moors. To the right, across the road, are some more baths, an unreconstructed underground warren of passages and hypocausts and small vaulted chambers with the standard starred windows. A little way ahead is a stretch of the old Moorish walls, agreeably lined with a long strip of garden. Here you pass statues of two of Cordoba's most notable citizens: first Averroes (d.1198), Arab scholar and translator of the Greek classics, then Seneca, the first-century Roman philosopher, playwright and tutor of Nero. Beside Seneca is the Almodovar Gate, the second along this stretch of wall, inside which lies one of the most pleasurable experiences in Andalusia.

Cordoba is the best of the three great Moorish cities for casual strolling. The area you are about to enter — the Jewish quarter — is larger than its Seville counterpart, yet is gathered within easy reach of the mosque. And the patios, the main delight of urban Andalusian architecture, are more plentiful and varied than in Seville, and more visible than the secret gardens of Granada. Much has been commercialized, to be sure, but it is hard to cavil at the consequent neatness and colour, and at the availablity of restaurants and romantically cloistered inns.

A short walk down Maimonides street, to the right inside the Almodovar Gate, leads to Andalusia's only surviving synagogue. It is now in sad shape: yet it is an interesting survival – as is a Jewish quarter at all – when you consider that Isabella expelled the Jews in 1492. After this excursion, return to the gate and head straight on down Fernandez Ruana street until it widens into a little square. On your right is the flaking façade of the Casa del Indiano, with its plain fourteenth-century Moorish structure embellished with late fifteenth-century Christian ornamentation.

A little further on is the massive convent of Christ Crucified. This is hard to enter, both because it is *in clausura* and because the entrance is not easy to find, being an anonymous door in a plain building to the right of the church's façade. But persist, and ring the bell, since the church itself is open to visitors. Beyond it – and beyond bounds – you will glimpse a pretty patio where white arches rest on a motley collection of Roman, Visigothic and Muslim capitals. And inside the tall one-roomed church is one of the finest coffered roofs in Andalusia . . . enormous, recessed, unpainted, but magnificently carved.

A tortuous route from the convent leads to Andalusia's best-hidden Arab bath. Its entry is through an antique shop in the narrow Velasquez Bosco, opposite the Calle de Las Flores, worth visiting itself for its wealth of flowers. The bath – the oldest in Andalusia – has a tiny open patio surrounded by keyhole arches resting on capitals dating from before AD 1000, all different. Behind is a barrel-vaulted stone sauna, and around the patio were formerly other rooms, now incorporated into the surrounding buildings.

Continue down Velasquez Bosco and you are soon back at the mosque. All the area of this walk has been a maze of cobbled alleyways, with white walls interspersed with stretches of stone and faded brick, and wrought-iron grille-work over windows, and around balconies and entrances. Peer into every doorway as you pass, since most lead into patios – large or small, plain or arcaded, tiled or leafy. The pattern of these courtyards is inherited, via the Moors, from the Roman ground-plan for a house, and they are celebrated in full during the Festival of the Patios in early May. Within them, beneath the palms and cypresses or the awnings that are spread in summer, amidst glinting ceramics and cascading flowers, and sounds of water and song-birds, you may catch a glimpse of how the Moors lived.

In a bar hereabouts I was served the definitive mug of *gazpacho* . . . icy, breathtakingly sharp, invigorating, almost chewy, pungently anti-social. This liquid food, compounded of bread and garlic, oil and vinegar, onions and cucumbers, tomatoes and peppers, has fuelled peasants and paupers and private soldiers through the southern Mediterranean, in different versions, since the Roman Empire and before. It was doubtless bread soaked in *gazpacho* that the soldier gave Christ on the cross. Cordoba has other more local delicacies too: frogs with tomatoes, hare with vinegar sauce, spiced ox-tail stew, fried sucking-pig.

Half a kilometre north-east of the mosque is the Archaeological Museum, in a much-restored but still attractive palace with patios, pools and gardens. Its many halls contain some fine exhibits among the predictable Roman statues and columns: notably an exquisite mudejar well-head, an engaging Iberian lion, a tenth-century bronze and enamel deer (looking more like a horse) from the palace of Medina Azahara (see below), and many splendid mosaics. There are also a number of iron braziers, similar to those used to this day for heating the houses in the small villages. They are set under the table, and account for the mottled and unhealthy legs of the peasant women who sit around them.

Zig-zagging another half kilometre south-east, you soon reach the Calle San Fernando, which runs north–south outside another stretch of wall. Turn right down

Cordoba: mudejar windows in a partial *alfiz* or frame of plasterwork.

Left **Justice in a baroque frame: the church of La Merced, Cordoba.**

Right **This flower-filled patio in Cordoba illustrates the central role of the courtyard in Moorish architecture.**

it, then left along a small street signposted to the Museo de Bellas Artes. Housed in a fifteenth-century hospital hidden behind a modern façade, the museum contains works by a number of Cordoban painters, of whom the best known is Valdés Leal, plus some attributions to more famous non-Cordobans such as Ribera, Zurbarán and Murillo. The two finest paintings are Goya's portraits of Charles IV (1784–1819) and his wife. They were not the most brilliant of Spanish monarchs – and Goya has let it show.

Outside the museum, and stretching down to the river, is a long narrow square with an indefinable charm that makes it one of the pleasantest spots in Cordoba. Its name, the Plaza del Potro, refers to the sprightly statue of a colt on top of the 1577 fountain at the upper end. A little further down on the right is the plain wooden door and lintel of the Posada del Potro, one of the few surviving examples of a medieval inn. It was well-known in the sixteenth century, and is referred to by Cervantes in *Don Quixote*. It is now occupied by the Delegacion de Cultura, but you can peer through the gateway at the cramped little yard, with its heavy wooden balconies and a drinking-trough fed by a lion-headed down-pipe. In a city of elaborate patios, the Posada's massive simplicity offers a satisfying contrast.

In the lower half of the plaza is a bar with outdoor tables which I remember well from my last visit: not so much for the montilla I was served there, but for the weather. It was ten o'clock at night and dark, but the heat of the August sun still radiated from the paving stones. When I inadvertently brushed one, picking up some fallen object, it was almost too hot to touch. I was reminded of Susa, ancient capital of the Persian Empire; according to Alexander the Great's historians, the place was so hot that snakes and lizards dared not cross the road at midday 'for fear of being burnt alive'.

If you return to the Calle San Fernando, the next right-hand turn to the north leads through an archway to the convent of San Francisco. This was originally founded in the thirteenth century, although its decorations are much later. The west door is flanked by curious pilasters, which look as if a whole series of these features have been superimposed, one upon another. To the left is a huge ruined cloister, of which only two rows of mouldering brick arches remain, topped by a similarly unkempt belfry. The interior of the church is structurally plain, but between the pillars and around the domes is a frothy eruption of decoration in the churrigueresque style. Here it can be studied more easily than elsewhere, especially in the last two chapels on the right, where the looping and whorling plasterwork, painted in blue and gold, dances close above your eyes.

Most of the other sights of Cordoba are too far to reach on foot, especially in summer, although the first of them is still quite close. Half a kilometre north-east from San Francisco is the Plaza Mayor, or Plaza de la Corredera. Dating from the late seventeenth century, it is remarkably complete – and also remarkably shabby for so trim and civilized a city. Instead of the stone glories of its equivalent in, say, Salamanca, it is of crumbling brick, with continuous arcading below and three storeys of tenements above. There is no ornamentation except where a couple of palaces interrupt the circuit, and only a few splashes of geraniums on the tottering balconies to vary the façades. The central expanse is similarly bare. The result is either depressing or exhilaratingly authentic, according to taste. In its heyday the plaza was used for bullfights. More recently it was a market. It has yet to find a new role.

The church of San Pablo lies a further half kilometre north. Dating from 1241, it is a magnificent jumble of architectural styles. The north door is richly baroque, but the interior is basically romanesque with Moorish elements superimposed, notably the fine ceiling (1537) and some caliphal capitals. These may deceive you into thinking you are in a converted mosque, but in fact the Christian builders employed mudejar craftsmen and used materials from the ruins of Medina Azahara. The mudejar elements are most vivid in the sacristy, with its elaborate plasterwork, tiles and a Moorish dome.

Continue east up San Pablo street, and within a couple of hundred metres an alley on the right gives a

___

Roman head in the Museo de Bellas Artes, Cordoba.

glimpse of the Palace of Villalones. The façade is modest but satisfying: a simple doorway surmounted by a rather more elaborate renaissance window, and at the top a delightful arcaded loggia. Turn left at the next intersection, by the church of San Andres, and you soon reach the Viana Palace.

This fills an entire block, and is a mind-boggling demonstration of the Muslim genius for secreting a lush and elaborate lifestyle within a humble exterior – and of how this genius survived long after the Moors had gone. Inside the bare façade are no less than 13 patios and 181 rooms. The site and perhaps the ground-plan are those of the palace of the last caliph, but the present building dates from the seventeenth century. To wander from shade to light, from marble to flowers and foliage, and from urns and statues to fountains and ornamental pools, is to appreciate how the Moors combined architecture with horticulture: not by placing a palace within a garden as at, say, Versailles, but by integrating the garden within the palace.

All the Viana patios are different, some tall, some low, some simple, some elaborate. Their walls are covered with plumbago or jasmine, or the musk rose *Banksiae*, a stone chest is filled with arum lilies, there are tubs of margaritas, plantations of oranges and tangerines, and a bougainvillea with a trunk the thickness of a man's body. There is also a museum of guns, swords and porcelain. Under your feet are patterned cobbles that ape Roman mosaics, and over the garden walls you can catch fleeting glimpses of the outside world from which the caliphs and grandees so successfully isolated themselves.

From the Viana it is a short walk north to the oldest church in Cordoba, Santa Marina, dating from the city's reconquest in 1236. It is one of my favourites, because of its simplicity. The north door, massively gothic, wrenches you abruptly back from the fripperies of Moorish decor to the more sombre vision of Christianity; and inside the austerity continues, with a

Santa Ana, with the Virgin and Christ, outside the church dedicated to her in Cordoba.

tall gothic nave and aisles that are almost entirely without decoration. The only elaboration is a flurry of Arabic plasterwork around the entrance to the sacristy, or Orozco Chapel, and *trompe l'oeil* paintings on the dome inside.

Outside Santa Marina is a statue to the bullfighter Manolete, born here and killed by the bull Islero in 1947. Beyond him is the convent of Santa Isabel, with a pleasing whitewashed patio, and beyond this again – a couple of hundred metres south and then round a corner to the west – is a very different statue, which you should try to visit twice, by day and by night: the Cristo de los Faroles. In a long cobbled yard, a small limp Christ hangs on a large plain cross, surrounded by eight lanterns. There is nothing else. The surrounding walls are white and almost windowless. The façade of the church that Christ faces is as plain as any in Andalusia. At night the effect is even more poignant. The dim light of the lanterns barely reaches the surrounding walls, and the Christ hangs there in lonely limbo, a man of shadows.

A few kilometres outside Cordoba is the great palace-complex of Medina Azahara, the City of the Flower, where a dream of Cordoba's heyday is being realized, year by year, on a dusty hillside. The Flower was the favourite wife of Abderrahman III, who began the Medina at her suggestion in 936, with money inherited from one of his concubines. It is a piquant thought, that a caliph's harem should include a grateful millionairess, but contemporary documents confirm that it was so.

Cordoba was then approaching the very acme of its glory – its Caliphate was the richest state in the west and ruler of most of Spain – and the Medina was constructed on a scale and to a level of luxury that aroused admiration even in Constantinople. The first phase of construction lasted 25 years and employed 10,000 men, 2600 mules and 400 camels. There were 4300 columns, for which some of the capitals were brought from Carthage and other ancient cities (and have travelled further since, to the mosque, to Seville and elsewhere). It contained an *alcázar*, a mosque, baths, an aviary and zoo, a university, gardens, fountains and a pool of quicksilver to reflect the

Left Maimonides, one of Cordoba's distinguished sons. He wrote on medicine and Judaic law, and after exile to Cairo became physician to Saladin's family.

Above The good earth: to the south of Cordoba is the most heavily cultivated land in Andalusia.

127

sunset. In the palace, according to the writer Raleigh Trevelyan, was accommodation for a garrison of 1200 and a harem of 6300, a nice balance of power. The town centre covered over 100 hectares, and the outskirts stretched to Cordoba, 8 kilometres away.

The Medina's glories were short-lived. Only 74 years after its inception it was sacked by Berber mercenaries in the squabbles that abruptly broke up the Caliphate, and the ruins were pillaged for their materials and levelled. As at Italica outside Seville, cornfields grew over the site, until in 1944 the remains of the royal apartments were discovered under the dust, and a slow process of reconstruction began.

The Medina is reached via the old Seville road to the west, the C431, from which a signposted side-road winds up to the ruins through fields of fighting bulls and plantations of cork-oaks. Looking down from an upper terrace you can see the whole site below you, with the hot plain stretching away behind. Rising from the street plan are the reconstructed royal apartments, Hall of the Ambassadors and other state buildings, embellished with pillars of rose and black marble and walls of lacy stucco. The work progresses every year, but there is still little to see, and you may prefer to make this journey in your mind rather than by car: especially as the handsome fifteenth-century convent of San Jeronimo, on the hillside nearby, is closed.

Beyond the Medina Azahara turn-off, 17 kilometres further west, is the restored castle of Almodovar (yet another reputed repository for Pedro the Cruel's treasure), with the most aggressively spiky battlements in all military architecture. And further still is a side-turning to Hornachuelos, the setting for part of Verdi's *La Forza del Destino*. But our route into central Andalusia heads south from Cordoba, on the NIV to Seville. It leads through the most languid scenery in the south, an endless rolling expanse of cultivation. There are no trees, few houses, and the mountains for once are far away. In the spring these vast undulations are green with young corn and seedling sunflowers or tobacco. By autumn you are crossing something akin to a desert, for all its fertility — a succession of dunes of scorched earth, criss-crossed with the black-and-brown scars of the withering stubble.

After 50 kilometres you reach the River Genil, born in the snows of the Sierra Nevada, and the town of Ecija. This is one of the lesser-known treasures of Spain. Few tourists stop here, and no one with any sense does so in summer, when the place lives up to its nickname 'the frying-pan of Andalusia'. Yet Ecija is a baroque jewel. Its thicket of rose-red church-towers and the palaces that lie beneath them were almost all built in the eighteenth century, after the earthquake of 1755: and this gives the architecture an exceptional coherence. Moreover, many of the best buildings can be encompassed in a short circular stroll.

Ecija was the Roman Astigi, and the Genil is crossed by what was once a Roman bridge, though this and the walls were destroyed by the Cordoban Caliphate in a rebellion of 913. The town was captured by the Christians in 1240, after which its isolation made it a refuge for outlaws, notably a band known as the Seven Sons of Ecija. The town's signposting is still medieval, and it may be with some difficulty that you reach the Plaza Mayor. If so, you can recuperate in the small bar under the arches at the south-east corner where you can lean back against a Roman pillar, sip a bitingly cold manzanilla, and look out at the square from the shade.

It is a pretty sight. In the centre are oranges and palms, and around the sides are ranks of arcaded houses, old and new, culminating in the formal façade of the town hall at the far end. On the right, the church of San Francisco appears to be shouldering its way into the square through the intervening buildings, and round the corner to the left is the church of Santa Barbara (1790), with Roman columns beside its doors and richly-carved choir-stalls inside.

Walk on past Santa Barbara and turn left into Emilio Castelar. To the right at the end of the street is the palace of the Marqués de Peñaflor. The gateway (1721) is spectacular enough, in stone that modulates in colour from grey to pink to cream and in style from classical below to barley-sugar baroque above. But what really draws the eye is the balcony that curves

A welcome corner of shade in Ecija, nicknamed 'the frying-pan of Andalusia'.

away to the right. It is the longest in Spain, a delightful nonsense (since it gives on to a narrow street) with wrought-iron railings. The wall above is frescoed along its whole length, up to the eaves.

Inside, a small entrance patio leads to the old stables, with some of the former occupants' names over the mangers, and to a fine two-storeyed main patio, with a stone dado that bubbles up into cupola-shaped motifs. After this formality the elaborate double staircase comes as a shock. On the landing a froth of rococo stonework frames a *Virgin of the Rosary*, and more of it foams around the half-orange dome above.

Ahead of the palace is one of the most remarkable short streets in Spain, the Calle de los Caballeros, the Street of the Knights. It is lined with small palaces in a variety of styles. The renaissance Torres Cabrera at no. 41 dates from about 1530, which makes it older than most of the town's monuments; no. 43 has elaborate doorways and windows; and no. 52 sports an intriguing combination of pink brick walls with white panels, overhanging balconies and first-floor eaves, and a loggia above.

Then there are the churches. At the end of the Calle de los Caballeros is the mid eighteenth-century church of Santa Ana, with plain walls and a tower that is sober at the bottom and riotously baroque at the top, where pink-and-white stone alternates with the blue tiles that are the hallmark of Ecija. Back near the Peñaflor palace are two more churches. San Gil to the south was founded in 1479 but modified, like the others, after the earthquake. To the north is the great tower of San Juan, doyen of them all, standing in majesty over its ruined church, with the stone-and-tile decoration of the elaborate three-tier belfry spilling down the plain brickwork and curling round the window-frames.

From here you can ramble onwards, in a generally northerly direction, down alleys that beckon ahead of you, an amalgam of faded whitewash and pale brick, honey-coloured palace doorways and balconies picked out in yellow. There are no patios here and no gardens. Since leaving Cordoba, an hour away across the hot plain, we have passed in time from pre-Conquest to post-Conquest ... from Moorish elegance to the more solid manifestations of Christian confidence. Baroque

stone façades have replaced the slender keyhole archways, and the sky is full of Catholic belfries. Santa Cruz is hereabouts, another ruin, with a pair of tenth-century caliphal plaques on its detached bell-tower. Near it are San Pablo, with a baroque chapel, and, further west, Santa Clara, with a dome picked out in blue and cream. South from here is the Palace of Justice with its elaborate Moorish-style patio, beyond which you are back in the Plaza Mayor. On the far side of the square — but further afield — other red-and-blue towers, some with storks' nests, signal other churches. The most notable is Santiago, which dates from 1500 and has a fine Isabelline reredos and a renaissance patio.

When leaving Ecija, head south on the C430. Ahead of you are two small rural towns, Osuna and Estepa. Osuna has a market area north of the Plaza de España with handsome patios, and some fine rococo palace façades, rich in barley-sugar columns; above the town is a strange bare hilltop which warrants the drive up. It is occupied by the sixteenth-century college, now a school, impressively four-square with a good plain patio, and by the collegiate church of 1534–9. This is another plain building, but with plateresque doorways enhanced with terracotta reliefs and an elaborate plateresque patio inside. There is also a museum with paintings by Morales and Ribera.

Estepa is splashed onto the side of a hill steep enough to make an exploration of the town hazardous, with little to warrant it except the baroque Palace of the Counts and the luxury of walking on pavements of marble. Better to bypass the town and drive up to another strange hilltop. Like Osuna, Estepa was a Roman town, but the exploit for which it is remembered was earlier: rather than surrender to the Romans, the entire population chose death on a funeral pyre. The site of this heroism is eerie to this day: a high windy hill where the present and the past mingle disconcertingly. Amid the remains of the encircling walls, and the umbrella pines that sprout from the

---

Classical stonework and gothic woodwork: a palace doorway in Ecija.

The Plaza del Portichuelo, Antequera.

bleak turf, are two convents, a church and the great square keep of the castle. The convents are occupied, but no life is visible and the exterior walls are bare. The church is derelict, as is most of the castle. All these tall slabs of crumbling masonry confront you with a blank stare, like neglected sculpture in a park. Tombs gape among the relics of the castle walls, and a once-handsome octagonal mausoleum sheds its golden stones. The keep, unrestored but well-preserved, has so secretive an air that not even an arrow-slit relieves the solidity of its ramparts.

Part of the hilltop is paved, and there is a gazebo from which you can contemplate one of the many views which no visitor to Andalusia will forget. On one side are the jumbled terracotta roofs of the town. On the other are the high blue mountains which have been growing in front of you ever since you left Ecija, and will loom ever higher and more diverse over the next 50 kilometres, until you run up against the foothills of the great coastal range at Antequera.

For those who have, bravely, made this drive in summer, the lush green plantations in front of Antequera will beckon like an oasis. In fact there is a very welcome watering-hole here, a parador where you can sit by a swimming-pool, or enjoy local specialities such as *porra*, a particularly thick and virulent form of gazpacho. The town has the typical Roman and Moorish history, plus some relics from a much earlier period. It was taken from the Moors in 1410, reputedly with the first use of gunpowder in Spain, though this claim is also made elsewhere.

There is little of interest to lure you from your poolside, except a cluster of buildings at the far end of town. Beside the lower end of the castle is the early sixteenth-century church of Santa Maria, aggressively sited at the head of a flight of steps, and built from stone of a strident shade of red. The entrance front is worth a study. It is composed of a number of miniature façades within a series of recesses – something unique. Inside there is a Moorish-style roof, and a reredos two centuries older than the church. From here you can climb up through the terraced garden which now fills the bailey of the castle. When the French retreated in the Peninsular War, they intended to blow up the fortifications, as at Granada and elsewhere. But the soldier assigned to the task spent so long fondling a farewell to his mistress that he was captured before lighting the fuse. Even so, little military architecture remains except some stretches of wall and two towers, one of which, the Puerta de Malaga, has been converted to a chapel. The view is just about worth the stroll.

You can bypass Santa Maria on the way down, and walk through the Arco de Los Gigantes, erected in 1585 but embodying stones with Roman inscriptions. To the right at the bottom is the leafy little Plaza del Carmen, beyond which a short street leads on to the edge of town. At the end is an agreeable jumble of walls and roof-tiles barely recognizable as a small church. This is El Carmen, with a baroque interior. The reredos is intimidating, the architectural details are fussy, and the painted walls are reminiscent of Victorian wall-

Roofs of gold, walls of ivory in Antequera.

paper: but the *artesonado* roof is a good example.

Sixteen kilometres to the south of Antequera is the El Torcal Park, an area where wind erosion has created a very strange landscape. Take the C3310 – a spectacular road running down to the coast – and bear right after 12 kilometres. This is a region of weirdly convoluted red rocks, interlaced with paths where you can appreciate other details of the scenery: birds of prey, spring flowers such as the light red *Paeonia broteri* and the jade green *Helleborus foetidus*, lizards and the occasional scorpion, and sweeping views of mountains and the Mediterranean.

There are dramatic stones of a different kind east of Antequera on the Granada road. On the left is a group of dolmens, or burial chambers under mounds, dating from about 2500 BC. The Menga, less than a kilometre out of town, is the most elaborate, and like Stonehenge gives an indication of the astonishing feats achieved by megalithic man: the stone slabs covering the narrow passage-like tomb average 180 tonnes in weight. The Viera chamber is nearby and the Romeral another 2 kilometres further on. Beyond the dolmens an immense crag juts from the plain beside the road, shaped like a reclining face. This is the Lovers' Peak, from the top of which, according to a poem by the English poet Robert Southey, a Christian knight and a Moorish maiden leapt to their death, wrapped in each other's arms.

Ten kilometres further on an equally dramatic cluster of peaks rises from the valley floor, with traces of habitation visible on the one on the right. This is the acropolis of Archidona. From below it looks fatiguingly remote, but you should resist the temptation to pass by. The approach road, signposted to the Sanctuario, winds up and up, finally passing the towers of the outer bailey, and ending outside the entrance to a church. Inside is a real treasure, a tiny mosque whose architecture spans a period from before the Moorish conquest to after the Reconquest. Its very existence was barely known until recently, since the

Santa Maria la Mayor, Antequera, a hall-church of 1503–50.

Wafer-thin brickwork in the Plaza del Portichuelo, Antequera.

Muslim heart was overlaid with Christian clothing, and yet its structure is astonishingly intact. The mosque dates from the ninth or tenth century, and the first three arches inside the door are older still – Visigothic – perhaps from an earlier Christian church on this site. The two beyond are vaulted and stand on seventeenth-century Christian columns; elsewhere are a baroque dome, a Moorish keyhole arch, and a fifteenth-century ceramic font donated by Ferdinand and Isabella. On the right is the former *mihrab*, which was later adapted to an altar to the Virgin. Outside is a little seventeenth-century courtyard with brick arches on two sides, and above are the scant remains of the castle, the scene of fierce fighting between Arab and Christian, and previously between Arab and Arab. It is set on one of the most needle-tipped pinnacles in Andalusia, and you will need to watch your step, or you will find yourself emulating Southey's lovers.

Archidona's eighteenth-century Plaza Ochavada, a perfect octagon.

The town below the hill contains little of interest except an architectural curiosity, the Plaza Ochavada. This alluring octagon is surrounded with a continuous row of late seventeenth-century houses in white picked out with red brick. Occasional arches pierce the lower storeys and loggias top the façades. Sitting among the flowerbeds in the square, you feel you are inside a small but elaborate bull-ring (which it once was), or a large dolls' house.

Continuing east from Archidona towards Granada, turn left at Salinas, on the C334 heading north. This is a small, rough road that winds through rolling country planted with olives and almonds. Goats graze the occasional patches of stubble, prosperous white farmhouses stand here and there, and the colour of the earth between the olive trees changes from red to ochre to white and back again. As your car switchbacks up and down, you become aware of the barometric principle of Andalusian agriculture: when the road dips you find yourself among cornfields, as it rises you are driving through olive plantations, and when it climbs higher still you emerge into rough scrub with rocks and pines.

On one of the long descents, into a huge bare valley among the hills, there is a sudden glimpse of a lake ahead, and of a town high above it. This is Iznajar, and the lake is man-made: down on the finger-shaped sandbanks the rows of swamped olive-stumps march out into the water, until only their heads are visible. Beyond the second of two bridges there is a dramatic view of the town, dominated by its castle and sixteenth-century church. The zealous can drive up, with considerable difficulty, to a belvedere on the hilltop, overlooking the castle and the lake.

From Iznajar the road winds up through endless olive plantations to Rute, which has no merit except a distillery. The next town, Lucena, is notable only for its gigantic churches and for the production of the great Ali Baba jars in which montilla wine, made nearby, is fermented and stored. Up in the centre of the town is the Plaza Nueva, the best place to park your car and find a café. At one end of the square is the fifteenth-century church of San Mateo, with a low, almost Italianate façade. There are aggressively tiled roofs on the narrow tower and sanctuary, in orange, red and blue with spikes on the corners and pinnacles, like a pair of hats for polychrome porcupines.

Behind the church to the right is a glimpse of the only two surviving towers of the castle. Boabdil, the last Moorish king of Granada, was imprisoned in the octagonal one for a period during the Reconquest, after his capture by the Christians. They then let him go, rightly guessing that this would cause civil war among the Moors. It seems typical of his general bad luck that he should have been locked up in so drab a town.

Driving up past the castle you will find a clutch of churches on the upper rim of the town. The best of them is the Hospital de San Juan de Dios, with a remarkable two-level west doorway of painted stone. Inside is a patio with the remains of wall-paintings,

and a finely-carved reredos. There is something a little ironical about Lucena's plethora of Christian churches (there are others at the bottom of the hill), since the town was a self-governing Jewish community under the Muslims, until the Jews were driven from the region by their masters, and later from the whole of Spain by the Christians.

From Lucena, take the C327 north if you wish to visit Cabra, 10 kilometres away. Once a Roman town, and later one of Andalusia's ten bishoprics in Visigothic days, it used to be famous for its marble quarries, which provided many of the pillars for the mosque at Cordoba. It was also the birthplace in the ninth century of the blind Arab minstrel Mukkadam, a forerunner of the troubadours of Provence. There is a festival here in September, in which the Most Holy Virgin of the Sierra is escorted through the streets by horsemen in costume. The celebrations continue for days, and include parades, bullfights and a battle of flowers.

All that survives of the castle is the massive keep, which now overlooks the patio of a seminary: it has been domesticated, with cosy eaves masking the sharp-toothed merlons and a pair of Moorish double windows piercing the bare walls. In front of the seminary is the baroque church of the Asuncion, with a richly rococo south door. It stands on a pleasant square, from the far end of which there is a view over the lower town and the surrounding countryside.

There is a more rewarding walk into the old Moorish section of the town, up an alleyway, the Cuesta de San Juan, which runs off to the left at the bend of the road back towards Lucena. Fork left halfway up: the going is steep and rough underfoot, but delightful, with arches bridging the narrowing walls and tiny windows punctuating the whitewash. Here there are fewer of the great wrought-iron grilles that are so common elsewhere: everything is plain and miniature and ancient.

At the top of the alley is a little square, across which is the whitewashed north wall of San Juan Bautista, a tiny ex-mosque. (If it is closed, knock on the door to the right of the classical west entrance.) The vaulting over the brief nave and aisles is primitive, with round

Above From this clay, around the town of Lucena, are made the huge *tinajas*, the Ali Baba jars in which the local wine is fermented and stored.

Right The heart of Andalusia, west of Cabra. For two centuries this was disputed territory between the Christians and the Moors.

arches on plain piers. Behind one of the pillars near the altar is a wheel of bells for use during the various stages of the Mass. In the sacristy in the south-east corner – now a junk-room – is a Visigothic stele with a misspelt inscription recording that a church, traditionally this one, was consecrated in 590. There is a little gallery at the west end of the nave, but otherwise nothing interrupts the monastic compactness of the white-washed masonry. In a land of elaborate decoration, the bareness of this small place is very endearing.

Thirty kilometres east of Cabra is Priego de Cordoba. Like Ecija, it is a handsome mid Andalusian town that no one visits. The castle sits unaggressively in the middle of the old sector and you can park your car outside it (follow signs to the Zona Historica), in a little park with a bar at one end. The castle has a well-preserved curtain wall, massive but compact enough to stroll around in five minutes. The entrance, to the left of the central tower facing the park, is a gothic doorway leading to two keyhole arches, with a slot between them for the administration of unwelcoming objects or fluids from above. Inside is a garden with fruit-trees, roses and an arbour. Amid such domesticity, it is almost a shock to see the great square keep looming ahead.

Opposite the bar is the church of Santa Maria de la Asuncion, with a pleasingly jumbled exterior and a bruisingly rococo interior. The tiled roofline heaves and juts, with dormer windows, a miniature belfry, a plain stone tower that looks as though it was borrowed from the castle, and a cheeky phallic pinnacle at the east end wearing a green-and-white tile condom. Inside, you will need to take a deep breath before entering the sanctuary. Dating from 1782, it gives the visitor the sensation of being inside a wedding-cake. Octagonal and three-layered, its upper parts are exhaustively stuccoed with mixed fruit, wildlife, and figures of the four apostles. The rest of the church's

Priego de Cordoba. Its gracious palaces and baroque churches were a product of the silk trade in the eighteenth century.

interior is plain by comparison, with flat octagonal pillars and round vaults. There is an English grand-father clock (a culture-shock, but a not uncommon sight in Spanish churches) and a better-than-average reredos, with well-proportioned figures in subdued colours.

Behind La Asuncion is the old Arab quarter, signposted as the Villa Artistica. It is rimmed by a promenade running around the walls, with views over the olive-flecked hillsides. Between the compacted houses the alleys narrow to clefts, some so slender that you can touch the walls on either side. There is nothing artística about this style of architecture, quite the reverse: it is the way poor people lived 500 years ago. Walking down one of these cool dark passageways is like threading a needle, and gives immediacy to Christ's saying about the rich man and the camel.

Returning to La Asuncion, those gluttonous for more pastry-cook stucco-work can walk to the end of the park and turn left. After a few hundred metres, the elaborate two-tier west front and belfry of the chapel of the Aurora, built in 1771, give a warning of what lies within. A little further, down an alley to the right, is the less cloying church of San Francisco. Its façade, on a pleasant square lined with young acacias, is more restrained, with unusual geometric flushwork on the walls and a loggia above. The interior is more florid. The reredos is of the type occasionally seen in Spanish churches, where the deity lurks inside a sort of carved grotto (a camarín). There are sculptures by Montañés, but the chapel of the Nazarene should only be entered by those with a strong stomach, or doing a thesis on rococo decoration. Apart from the plasterwork, there is a reredos covering three sides of the chapel, ornamental balconies on the walls and a flamboyant pulpit supported on a winged caryatid.

Back at the castle, the street that continues the line of the park leads in a few hundred metres to the big square in front of the town hall. To the left, at the corner of the square, is the Calle del Rio, the most gracious street in Priego, its languid curves bordered with pavements of red, white, black and grey marble. It is lined with palaces, of which the best are on the left. Their façades are basically plain, but elaborated

with plateresque detailing, lush baroque doorways and balconies, and intricate grille-work. One palace has an open loggia; some have ceramic tiles around their windows. You can picture the local grandees vying with each other – not too strenuously – in the decoration of their homes, back in the peaceful days of the Bourbons, when the town was enriched by the immigrant Catalans who founded the local textile industry.

The church of El Carmen is on the left, with a classical belfry and a sober west door. The interior is also simpler than many seen elsewhere, consisting of a small whitewashed nave with high galleries. There is another *camarín*, containing the Virgin standing on a half-moon, as in many paintings of the period. Beyond the church you soon hear the sound of falling water. The river which once followed the course of this street, and was used to drive water-mills, has since been harnessed to form the fountains at the top.

They lie above a flight of steps, in a small square surrounded by eight huge plane-trees which do their best to hide the modern buildings around. Neptune presides over the main fountain of 1782, where nearly 200 jets, many with grotesque faces, pour their water into an octagonal pool. The upper fountain of 1753 is less formal, with pebbles shining through water as clear as *vino verde*, and a Virgin, flanked with mythological figures, in front of a rusticated stone wall.

The route back to Cordoba is the N321 out of Priego to the north, past the entrance to the old royal slaughterhouse. The road leads down a narrow valley lined with apple-trees, an unusual sight in these parts. Olives look down on these interlopers from the slopes above, which steepen into a gorge. On the left rise the towers and walls of an eerily isolated hilltown, Fuente Alhama, beyond which the landscape flattens and withers, until the only surviving greenery in summer is in the leaves of the tamarisks and eucalyptus along the river. And the inhospitality of this hinterland is

Andalusia's fountains continue the tradition of the Moorish love of water. This one is in Priego.

typified by the lone watch-towers on the hilltops. Then the wilderness softens into broad rolling plantations of olives, which give way in turn to vineyards. These are set on blinding white soil as at Jerez, and their grapes are taken to Montilla, a few kilometres to the west, to make a sherry-like wine.

Some montilla wine goes through a *solera* process similar to that of sherry, and is made from one of the sherry grapes (Pedro Jimenez), but there is a major difference between the two types. Montilla is unfortified. The fiercer inland temperatures give the grapes a higher sugar content, and the must froths feverishly in open earthenware jars to reach a natural strength of 16° of alcohol. At this strength, and in this heat, you would expect the resulting wine to be coarse. But it is wonderfully civilized and delicate, clear and fragrant, perhaps slightly grapier than sherry when drunk young, and without doubt one of the world's great aperitifs. The sherry people have paid it the ultimate

Neptune fishing in the Fuente del Rey, Priego. A larger version of this statue stands near the Prado in Madrid.

compliment by stealing its name: amontillado means sherry in the montilla style. The town of Montilla has its *bodegas*, and wine connoisseurs may want to make the detour south-west from Espejo (see below).

Some 30 kilometres from Priego, the Cordoba road passes the village and fine castle of Luque, then rounds a corner to reveal Baena ahead, heaped on a dun-coloured hill, with its church dominating the old town above, and the new town sprawling below. The main monuments are as usual at the summit of the hill, but are barely worth the drive: the sixteenth-century church was ruined in the Civil War (though it is now being restored), there is little left of the once-proud castle (the key to which is obtainable from the town hall), and the convent is closed to visitors, permitting only a glimpse through its gate of the pretty patio within. But it is worth turning off the highway into the old town and taking one of the streets that girdle the hill halfway up. You will pass a succession of hand-some houses, bourgeois mansions from the renaissance period and earlier, with jutting Moorish-style windows capped with tiled canopies. Not very many towns in Andalusia remain as dignified and unspoilt.

By now the mountains have withdrawn behind you, and a lush valley runs beside the road, green with gardens even in summer. Beyond are the rolling expanses of wheat and sunflowers which sweep from here to the Guadalquivir. Rising from them like an island from calm seas is the walled hummock of Castro, with its church tower at the summit pointing to the sky. The best view of it is from the highway, but the lower town offers an agreeable ten-minute stroll, if you can stand the smell of olive oil. Drive through the drab suburbs, past the castle which unusually squats down here beside the plain, and park in a pretty little square in front of the church of La Asuncion. The façade includes a once-fine plateresque doorway, but the church has a skewbald look overall, being compoun-ded of ochre stone, brick and whitewash. Around it spreads a pleasant network of cobbled streets, humbler, wider and quieter than at Baena, a restful combination of town and village. Ancient pillars bolster the street-corners, and great wrought-iron lamps hang overhead. Cervantes was a civil servant here in the late sixteenth century before he became a novelist, and was jailed for extortion (or rather for levying money from the wrong people – the clergy). His prison is still shown in the town hall, and it is possible that here was where he began *Don Quixote*.

Eight kilometres further on looms a final acropolis. Espejo is more conventionally composed than Baena, with a dapper castle on top, a little church below, and the rest of the town gathered round the hillside like a shawl. The colour scheme is familiar too – snow-white houses and golden castle. The latter can be reached by car, with difficulty, but it is the private residence of the Dukes of Osuna, and hence closed to tourists. It is compact, neat and well-preserved, with courses of brick and stone and double Moorish windows, a thicket of creeper loud with cicadas, and incon-gruously ferocious merlons round the top. If you hanker for a castle in Spain, you could do worse than this. Close below, the plain exterior of the church conceals a fourteenth-century interior in the Moorish style, with a reredos of the same period.

The final kilometres of the road to Cordoba run across the wide undulating plain which has long been the bread-basket and battle-ground of Andalusia. Over a couple of ridges to the left is Munda, where Caesar defeated the sons of Pompey in 49 BC, in a battle in which he afterwards said he was fighting not for victory but for his life; and further west is the site of Scipio's triumph over the Carthaginians in 210 BC. Subsequently this territory was for 200 years the no-man's-land between the Christian capital at Cordoba and the Moorish fastnesses in the central mountains. Now the corn tints the slopes, changing from iri-descent green through gold to striated brown as the summer advances. Soon a thin line of blue fills the horizon ahead – the Sierra Morena. As it grows, a smudge of white becomes perceptible, and in a few kilometres you are back in Cordoba, in powerful need of a bath, a change, and a glass of montilla.

Moorish warriors in Baena. For centuries this little town has produced some of the finest olive oil in Spain.

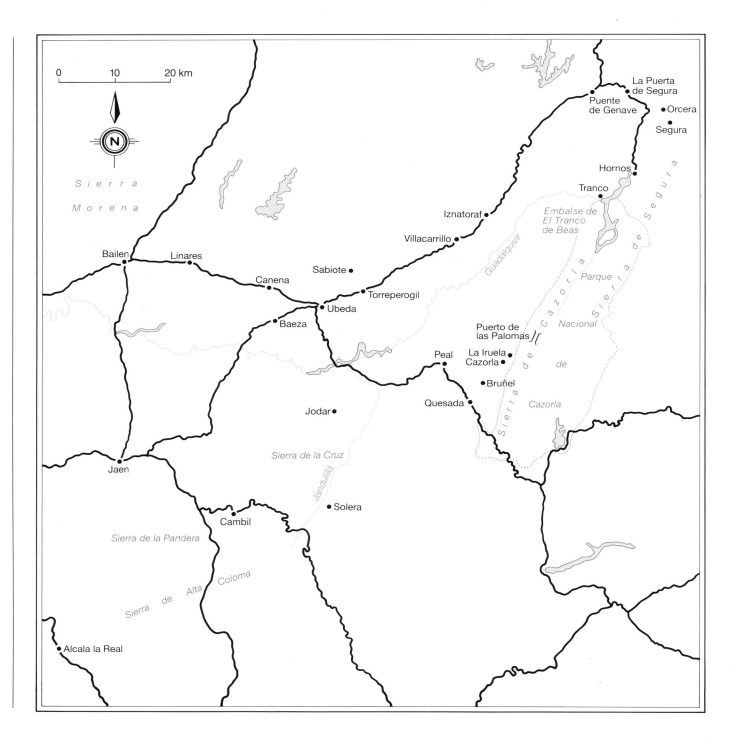

5
Jaen and the North-East

Jaen – Quesada – Cazorla – La Iruela –
Cazorla National Park – Segura – Ubeda – Baeza

Soy Baeza la nombrada,
Nido real de gavilanes.
Tinen en sangre su espada
De los Moros de Granada
Mis valientes capitanes.

Motto of the city of Baeza

(I am the far-renowned Baeza,
A royal falcons' brood.
Draw your sword, my valiant leaders,
Against Granada's Moorish raiders
And stain it with their blood.)

A glance at the map suggests that Jaen is as hard to reach as its name is to pronounce (it requires a dissyllabic guttural snort, whereas the best most foreigners can manage is an approximation of Tarzan's mate). But it is straightforward to drive there from Cordoba, east along the main Madrid road and then turning south at Bailen, or from Granada up the N323. It is a fine city in its own right, with a parador in the castle above, and is also a good jumping-off place for the treasure-houses of Ubeda and Baeza, and for the Cazorla National Park.

Jaen was a pre-Roman city, and the Carthaginian leaders took refuge here after their defeat by Scipio in 210 BC. It was too strong for the Romans to besiege, and only fell to them after the conquest of Carthage. Subsequently it was the capital of a small Moorish state. St Ferdinand captured it in 1246, and it became a key Christian base in the ring that encircled the Moors' last surviving kingdom of Granada for the next 250 years. It was sacked by the Moors in 1368 (and later by the French in the Peninsular War); and the redoubtable Isabella set out from here to bolster her husband, the other Ferdinand, when the going was getting tough in the final stages of the Reconquest.

Jaen's position at the crossroads between Castile and Andalusia – it's former Arabic name means caravan-route – is reflected in a look which has elements of both. The old town, still clustered within the remains of its walls amid a vast and empty countryside, has its southern whitewash half-eclipsed by the golden stone of the north: most notably in the case of the cathedral. This dominates a small square where you can sit among citrus trees and laurels and gaze upwards at the main façade. It is a fine building, one of the finest.

Built on the site of a mosque and of a gothic sanctuary, the main structure of Jaen cathedral was begun in 1540 and not finished for over 250 years. The design was by a local genius, Andres de Vandelvira, with many elements added by his colleagues and successors. Despite the long building time, the result-ing ensemble is coherent, balanced and wonderfully satisfying: opulently renaissance with barely a hint of baroque. The west façade is the most splendid part, with tall Corinthian columns between the doors, a unifying balcony running above them, statues and bas-reliefs, and elegant lanterns above the massive towers. Moreover, Jaen has one great advantage over the cathedrals of, say, France – its honey-coloured

Above After its recapture from the Moors, Jaen was a key frontier city – 'the guard and defence of the realm of Castile'.

Right Baroque athleticism on the cathedral at Jaen.

stone, modulating through many tones from sun to shade, glowing against the blue sky.

Lacking the sunshine, the interior is less rewarding, although still imposing. The clustered pillars and round vaults and domes are neither gold stone nor white, but grey, and the perspective of the nave is blocked (as so often) by the choir, which sits like a bulky cuckoo in the nest. Inside it, however, are some very fine sixteenth-century stalls, carved in high relief from dark walnut, some dating from the earlier church on this site. Continue past the choir to the east end of the cathedral, the oldest part, where the nobility of scale and proportion is most apparent. In a treasure-chest in the main chapel, locked away except on Friday afternoons, is the Santa Faz, one of St Veronica's various handkerchiefs (the best known of which is in Rome), and traditionally showing the face of Christ.

In the square opposite the cathedral's west front is the bishop's palace, charmlessly refurbished, and the seventeenth-century façade of the town hall. Leaving these on your left, head for the north-west corner of the square, where the Calle Maestra leads up into the oldest part of the town. Although modernized at this lower end, it has its own charm, with narrow alleys leading off to right and left, and it will take you to almost everything else worth seeing. On the right is the anonymous-looking Palacio del Condestable, with ceilings in the basement decorated in Moorish style, though they date from the fifteenth-century Christian occupation. Continue through the Plaza de la Audiencia, then bear right down the Calle de Virgilio Anguita to the fifteenth- and sixteenth-century church of San Bartolomé. This has a good *artesonado* roof, with typical star-burst panelling and tie-beams, but little else of merit: there are better things ahead.

Round the corner to the right at the next T-junction is the convent of Santa Clara. Enter the small modernized patio and ring a bell beside a door to your right. The guide will take you into the thirteenth-century church, through a loggia with the remains of paintings on the supporting pillars. The church is tall, almost gaunt, with another Moorish-style roof, and a high gallery at the west end. This has a fretted screen through which the nuns could watch the service (an unconscious echo of the fretted windows in Muslim streets, which protected women from the eyes of passers-by). The convent also has a spacious cloister, with vaulted arcading supported on double columns, but this is out of bounds.

From Santa Clara head uphill to the little Plaza de los Canos with a fountain of 1648, and turn down a right-hand alley to the nearby chapel of San Andres. This part of Jaen is very rewarding, with a number of fifteenth- and sixteenth-century palaces, and the chapel is equally rich. Dating from the sixteenth century, it has a classical doorway and a patio. The main glory of the interior is the elegantly vaulted chapel of the Immaculate Conception; this is fronted by an unusually fine wrought-iron screen of 1515, gilded and coloured, by Bartolomé of Jaen, the acknowledged master of this form of art, who designed the great screens in Seville and Granada. The chapel also contains a tiny, incongruous, Moorish door leading to the pulpit: and there are paintings attributed to Van Dyck and Dürer.

Uphill from the Plaza de los Canos is the church of San Juan, one of the city's oldest, with a tower where the city fathers had their first meeting after the Reconquest. Down the road to the right of its east end is the former convent of Santa Teresa, previously a Moorish palace. Its basement contains the much restored remains of an extensive system of Arab baths, with brick vaulting resting on stumpy stone pillars dating from the eleventh century.

Further along the Calle Santo Domingo, past the former convent of the same name with a 1578 doorway by Vandelvira, is my favourite church in Jaen, La Magdalena. To gain entry I had to make enquiries at a garage next door. The mechanic extricated himself from beneath a car, and led me down the street to a bar, where he introduced me to a man who had the key to the church. After a couple of beers he was happy to let me in and show me round. Santa Magdalena was once a

The ancient Greeks brought the olive to Spain. Now the olive trees fleck the hillsides in their millions, especially around Jaen.

mosque, and this shows immediately in the entrance patio, with its Moorish arches and an old ablution pool in the centre, fed by a constant stream which has a more visible outlet in the fountain in the square outside. This may have been the origin of the church's name – by recalling the flowing tears of Mary Magdalene – but other legends have evidently intervened, since the fountain is presided over by a stone dragon.

There are Roman gravestones let into the masonry of Santa Magdalena's patio, and the church's sixteenth-century interior contains a reredos by Jacobo Florentino, who worked with Michelangelo on the Sistine Chapel. The figures, in painted wood, include Christ with the two Marys, and are notable for their humanity and individuality (even a bit-player – a Roman soldier in armour – acts out a strong supporting role). The structure of the church is very plain, with strong rectangular pillars leading to simple vaulting, and some of the walls contain traces of early frescoes.

Around Santa Magdalena are the jumbled streets of the old Arab town, rising steeply to the crag on which stands the castle of St Catherine. Its towers are within easy arrow-shot, but the approach to it is by a 3-kilometre road that loops around the far end of the hill. Although Moorish in origin, on an earlier site, the castle was rebuilt by the Christians after they had captured it in 1246. It has been extensively patched up recently, and incorporates a modern parador in medieval style. There is an early fourteenth-century chapel in one of the encircling towers on the north side, but most of the rest is spanking new. You can walk along a footpath (unfenced) between the walls and a couple of detached towers to a rocky knoll at the further end of the hill, where there is a fine view back towards the castle, and an even finer vista out over the surrounding countryside, with its colour-washed earthen slopes studded with the flecks of a million olive trees. There is also a good view, from the road up to the castle, of the roofs of the town with the great gold cathedral in their midst.

While in Jaen you could sample the local cuisine. A typical meal hereabouts might start with *pipirrana*, a hotch-potch of tunny-fish, olives, egg and tomato, or *migas*, a sort of cous-cous but made with breadcrumbs or corn-flour, garnished with sausage. Main courses include the equivalent of *tête de veau* – calf's head fried in garlic – or *choto* (kid), or veal with olives, or game and trout from the mountains. The wine comes from areas nearby: red and white from Torreperogil, white from Bailen and rosé from Alcala la Real. The red is the best, firm and clean, one of few good reds in Andalusia.

From Jaen, a circuit into the mountains interposes some rural delights before returning to the architectural splendour of Baeza and Ubeda. Leave Jaen on the N321, heading east towards Granada and Almeria, and then fork right after 5 kilometres onto the N323 towards Granada. At first you find yourself among Jaen's famous olive plantations, one of the most characteristic visions of the south. Their slopes curve in a multitude of intersecting planes, as if by design, so that in the morning and evening the landscape is dappled with shadows. During the brightness of the day the earth, which is bare for hundreds of square kilometres, is patchworked with all the mineral colours of an artist's palette: umber and burnt sienna, ochre and pale terracotta and cadmium-white. Across this shimmering fabric roll the endless rows of trees, each line precise, but curving as the slopes curve, and merging with the other lines that swoop in from either side to form one of the richest patterns in all agriculture.

But the road south soon leaves the olives and plunges into a gorge, with high mountains in the distance on the left, and a ruined castle on the right. Ahead the way seems closed by the massif of the Sierra de la Pandera, topped by a peak as sharp as the Matterhorn: but before reaching it, 23 kilometres after leaving Jaen, turn left onto the N324. On the right, a little further on, are the remains of Cambil castle, one of the key Moorish fortresses barring the Christian advance from Jaen. Relying on its inaccessibility, it awoke one day – like Dien Bien Phu in the reconquest

---

Cambil. Its castle, previously thought impregnable, was pulverised by Isabella's cannon during the final advance on Granada.

ANDALUSIA

of French Indo-China – to find itself ringed with the artillery which Isabella had insinuated through the reputedly impassable ravines. The great lombards soon smashed down the hitherto impregnable walls, and the way to Granada lay clear.

Beside the road is a narrow green valley, a strip of fruit-trees and willows hugging a stream beneath the cliffs on either side, which heighten as the gorge narrows. The route climbs through cork forests, and after a little over 30 kilometres from the Granada road the C325 leads off to the left along the wider valley of the Jandulilla. This is an enchanted place, a level enclave between the encircling mountains, strangely deserted, with ruined farmhouses stranded among the pale white fields, and long ribbons of purple bugloss along the verges in May. To the right, through binoculars, can be seen the most vertiginous of all the local castles, Solera, on a needle of rock with a white necklace of houses below, jutting from the plain. Again the road threads a gorge and climbs a ridge – the Sierra de la Cruz – before running beneath a tottering golden cliff to Jodar.

There is nothing cultural to justify the short loop into Jodar: but for those in need of a rest and a drink there is a pleasant little square at the far end of town, with a pleasing church and an apologetic little castle, ruined and unrestored. On the square is a bar, loud with domino players. Having slaked your thirst here, you must make a choice of routes. To reach Cazorla, 50 kilometres away to the east, it is simplest to head north and pick up the C328, possibly making a trip from Peal to visit the 2000-year-old Iberian necropolis nearby. You can get the key for this from Peal's town hall, but unless you are a funerary obsessive the simple stone-lined burrow is barely worth the detour.

My own route to Cazorla is longer and looks alarming on the map, but is passable, and takes in a unique sight on the way . . . if you can find it. Turn east from Jodar towards Quesada. Thirty kilometres away across the plain the mountains face you like a wall, and as so often in Spain your gradual progress towards them across the dry flatlands acquires the drama of a heroic quest, or a pilgrimage, during which your eyes are fixed with increasing dedication on your goal.

At Quesada, there are scant remains of two castles and some town-walls, including a gateway, together with a gallery dedicated to a local twentieth-century artist, Rafael Zabaleta, a purveyor of flat earth-colours and chunky sub-Picasso figures. Two or three kilometres beyond the town, take the first road to the right, and then turn left, heading for Cazorla direct, rather than via Peal. You will soon pass a pair of signs indicating a historic site, with a track signposted to Bruñel running off to the left between them. Two hundred metres along this you must stop at a house on the left, the first old house past a modern bungalow, and ask for the key to the Roman villa (also available from the police in Quesada). Then continue up to the ridge immediately beyond, and park beside a ruined shack.

On the right is a fence with a gate in it. Inside, in a bare field, is the ground-plan of a large villa, dating from the second and third centuries, together with that of a fourth-century Christian basilica superimposed upon it. They were only discovered, by ploughing, in 1965. Apart from some pillar-stumps, little of interest survives except the mosaics on the floors and court-yards of the villa. These are extensive – the site covers $1\frac{1}{2}$ hectares – and are in various geometric and figurative designs, including lozenges, scrollwork and herringbone, some monochrome and some coloured. The most spectacular floor has medallions containing goddesses' faces and animals, among them a pert duck. There are finer mosaics elsewhere in Europe, including at Italica (see p. 32), but for the most part they are in museums, or under roofs, or covered in sand, or rigorously patrolled and often only visible over the shoulders of a gaggle of fellow-tourists. These at Bruñel are for you alone, deserted, enlivened by bright wild-flowers. The setting is a wilderness and the silence absolute. Even the least archaeologically in-clined will feel a frisson, I think, at standing here amidst this lonely relic of the Roman presence in Spain.

Cazorla, a dozen kilometres ahead, was another

So closely does Cazorla hug the mountainside, that when its bells ring the cliffs echo.

154

Roman settlement, and the Bruñel villa was doubtless the country mansion of one of its rich officials. Subsequently the town was a Moorish stronghold, and then the Christian capital of a frontier province. The two towers jutting above the town represent both periods. The nearer, La Yedra, is fifteenth-century Christian, and is known as the Tower with Four Corners – so-called because the other tower, El Moro, has five.

Cazorla is an agreeable little town, with a number of squares inserted among the crowded houses, like rooms where the furniture has been pushed back to make space for dancing. The furthest, the Plaza de Santa Maria, is the prettiest: follow signs to the church of the same name, by Vandelvira, now a handsome ruin which stands on one side of the oval plaza, overlooking the plane-trees and a renaissance fountain. Close behind the houses loom the mountains, and when the town bells ring the narrow valley echoes.

Extricating yourself from the town is the usual unsignposted nightmare. When you have finally emerged and oriented yourself, head east to La Iruela and the national park. La Iruela, a mere couple of kilometres away, is slapped against the side of a hill like a martin's nest, with a tiny but entirely satisfying castle, once owned by the Knights Templar, on a vertical crag at one end. This dramatic eyrie is accessible by car for those with steely nerves and a vehicle no larger than a perambulator. Take the Calle San Anton, which sneaks up behind a handsome renaissance building near the church: at the top there is just room to park beside a fountain and a solitary pillar. There is a bar on the left, with a fine view.

The castle's gatehouse and upper keep have been restored, but the other chunks of jagged masonry jut like carious teeth, black against the even blacker rock. The place looks villainous, haunted, dragon-infested. It belongs in the Rhineland, not under the southern sun. Inside the bailey is another sinister relic, a ruined renaissance church, like Santa Maria at Cazorla: these were two of the five thousand churches damaged or destroyed in the anti-religious back lash during the Civil War in the late 1930s. All around and above are the crags of the mountains, even more aggressive than the castle itself. Below is the golden immensity of the Guadalquivir valley.

A little way above La Iruela the road begins to climb and twist wildly as it scrambles over the Puerto de las Palomas, the Pass of the Doves, and thence down into the Cazorla national park which lies the other side. The park is encased between two long mountain ranges running almost north and south, in a narrow valley followed by the young Guadalquivir from its source at the valley head. Protected thus from the outside world, it is a natural retreat for various species of birds and mammals, including the mountain goat, the *Cabra hispanica*; also boar, moufflon, ibex, and such raptors as the goshawk, royal eagle, peregrine falcon and the rare and gigantic lammergeier, the *quebrantahuesos*, with a wing-span of 3 metres. The latter gets its name, the bone-breaker, from its practice of dropping bones from a great height in order to smash them open. The ancient Greek dramatist Aeschylus was killed by a similar bird, which dropped a tortoise on his head, mistaking the bald pate for a handy rock.

Of all this wildlife, what you are most likely to see as you thread your way through the dense stands of pine, mountain oak and juniper is the occasional herd of roebuck. Up a side valley to the right is a parador, agreeably styled like a mountain lodge. Though it has only a circumscribed view of the scenery, it offers a comfortable base for exploring the park. You may find partridge on the menu, and the staff will cook any trout you catch in the tributaries of the Guadalquivir (but you will need to have secured a licence in advance).

A long road runs along the left side of the Guadalquivir, which is joined at one point by the fast-flowing Borosa, the best place to hook your trout. After a few more kilometres a flash of blue ahead heralds the Tranco lake, a slim finger of water which fills the ravine below the tree-clad slopes. This could be Switzerland: green and silent and enclosed, a little claustrophobic. It is almost with a sense of escape that

Corn and olives in the Guadalquivir valley north of Cazorla.

Above **Tranco lake in the Cazorla national park, formed by damming the infant Guadalquivir.**

Right **Hornos, a fortified hill-village at the north end of the Cazorla national park.**

you climb out of the valley, 50 kilometres from the parador, taking the road that runs north from Tranco.

After a dozen kilometres a turning to the right leads past the walled town of Hornos, towering dramatically on the hillside, with the castle keep, white houses and ochre walls silhouetted against the dark forest behind. But an even more spectacular hilltown lies 15 kilometres ahead. This is Segura, which has given its name to the massif that walls-in the east side of the park. The town dates back to Phoenician times and before. Romans and Carthaginians fought for it, the Moors captured it in 781 and made it the capital of a kingdom, and under the Christians it became capital of the lands of the Order of Santiago. Later it held out against Napoleon's French invaders. The castle, high on a rocky cone above the houses, still echoes much of this history.

The castle key, which would not disgrace St Peter, is obtainable from the town hall, a miniature renaissance palace just inside the town gate, with an upper entrance leading directly on to the sentry's walkway along the walls. Cars can negotiate the bumpy but passable track that ends a little below the castle; but the remaining 100 metres must be walked, up a stiffish slope through a natural rock-garden of yellow and white rock-roses, thyme, and a pervasive pink succulent, while the view spreads and spreads below you.

With its yellow stone and smoothly rounded corners, the immaculately restored fortress looks like a talented youngster's sand-castle. Inside the courtyard is a delightful chapel, formerly a mosque, with a characteristic mix of styles: Moorish arcading in the chancel walls, a gothic chancel arch, and a barrel-vaulted roof. Outside, standing on the perimeter wall, you can hear every sound from the village that clusters below, compact and ancient, and all around you the ranks of olive trees march endlessly across the purple soil.

The church, built on the site of a temple, looks as military as the castle, with rough round buttresses and a spartan interior. In the square beside it is a handsome sandstone fountain carrying the arms of Charles V (1500–58), and nearby is a small Arab bath, heavily restored. The rest of the village is unspoilt, with

jumbled alleyways, steps and arches, and with occasional medieval mansions still carrying the coats of arms that attest the town's former glories. The people here are delightful, and slightly mad.

Continuing north, on the 8-kilometre stretch to Orcera, three *atalayas*, or watch-towers, jut irregularly from the rolling olive plantations to the left of the road. These towers were used for long-distance signalling, with fire by night and smoke by day, so to have three so close to each other seems excessive. Moreover these are of a distinctive design, tall and spindly like the towers of San Gimignano in Tuscany. Normally you can date these structures, especially along the coast, by their shape: the square ones are Roman, the round ones Moorish, and the broad, three-quarter circles Napoleonic.

Orcera is an unassuming little town, in which the best feature is the elaborate west door of the renaissance church of Our Lady of the Assumption. From here you can strike west along the C321 through La Puerta de Segura, and pick up the main road (N322) just east of Puente de Genave. Ubeda is 77 kilometres to the south-west, with three sights worth pausing for en route. About halfway, a small road to the right leads up to the ruined fortress of Iznatoraf, which even in this country of hilltop fastnesses is one of the dizziest eyries of all. Shortly thereafter you pass Villacarrillo, with painted vaults in the nave of a church built by Vandelvira. Finally, 10 kilometres short of Ubeda is a right-hand turn-off to the castle of Sabiote.

The castle is ruined and locked. You can get the key from the town hall, and you may be accompanied, as we were, by a policeman as a guide. (Contrary to some visitors' preconceptions, the Spanish police are extremely cooperative, and far readier to show off their monuments than are the clergy to aid admission to theirs.) Our escort cheerfully led us through the weedy wilderness that surrounded the castle, shrugging off the damage to his immaculately pressed trousers. '*Muy*

Segura de la Sierra. As in other mountain villages in Jaen province, one of its fiestas is an *encierro*, when bulls are run through its streets.

valiente!' he chirped admiringly, as my diminutive wife hopped from tussock to tussock, avoiding the puddles left by a recent storm. Ahead of us, the low sixteenth-century fortifications showed little of their Moorish origins, and the interior was a crumbling shell, with fireplaces clinging to the floorless walls, and traces of hall and kitchen, stables and postern gate: romantic, but meagre fare.

Ubeda runs Arcos (see p. 82) very close as my favourite town in Andalusia. And, indeed, it is no fair contest between the two, since they are so different. Arcos is the perfect macrocosm of a Moorish hill-village. Ubeda is Christian, and northern, and with the rich dignity of a city: a stunning agglomeration – one of the finest in Spain – of noble renaissance palaces within a small compass. It was once an Iberian settlement, and was a prosperous centre under the Moors, from whom it was twice captured by the Christians, the second time in 1234. Many of the nobles who accompanied the conquering St Ferdinand on this campaign took up residence here and built themselves mansions. Another reason for its wealth is the fact that the town, like Jaen, lies on an old trade route between the Christian and Moorish parts of Spain, which accounts for the mingling of architectural styles.

Coming into town, pause in the Plaza de Andalucia, characterized by a medieval clock-tower with a seventeenth-century cupola. There are some attractive houses here, of which my favourite is a tiny one on the west side, only 3 metres wide, with an open loggia above supported by a single pillar. On the north-east corner of the square is the church of La Trinidad, with two heavy baroque doorways. Walk north past its west end, up the Calle de la Trinidad, and you soon pass the palace of Los Bussianos on the right, with handsome first-floor windows set in a plain façade. Nearby is the church of San Nicolas, for which you can get the key from the house to the right.

The magnificent west door was designed by Vandel-

Cypresses are a rare sight in Andalusia. Much more typical are the rows of olive trees visible on the hill behind.

vira in 1566. It leads into one of the oldest interiors in Ubeda, begun in the thirteenth century and built over the next two hundred years. It is pure gothic and very simple, but its chief glory is again later and more elaborate: a chapel on the north side, also by Vandelvira. It is heralded by an extraordinary floor-to-ceiling entrance of 1537 in the plateresque style, and closed off by one of the best wrought-iron screens in Andalusia. This is plain below, but above is a coat of arms, supported by figures and dragons and topped by the Virgin and a choir of angels playing musical instruments. All is in flat relief, and coloured in muted tones of pink and blue and red. On a more macabre note, the four bands of decoration on each of the screen's main pillars are formed by rows of skulls.

Retrieving your car from the Plaza de Andalucia, drive east down the Corredera de San Fernando, and bear right. In about a kilometre you will come to a small road junction, on the right side of which is one of the city's gates, the thirteenth-century Puerta del Losal. This is a Moorish survivor, built at right-angles to the wall, and thus compelling any attackers, whose shields would be on their left arms, to expose their unprotected right flank to the unfriendly attentions of the defenders on the battlements.

The road ahead circles the outside of the city, with the open plain on the left. About a kilometre further on, at a shady little park with a fine view, turn right down the Calle Baja del Salvador. This leads to one of the handsomest small squares in Spain, the Plaza Vazquez de Molina, lined with a wonderful confection of palaces and churches in warm gold stone. A stroll around this little space alone warrants a visit to Ubeda.

It also contains the best place to stay. The long low building on the right, formerly the palace of the Condestable Dávalos, is now a parador. Unlike the church next to it, the façade of the palace is a hymn to the virtues of simplicity. Its beauty lies in its proportions, since few details relieve the tight-lipped severity. The only concession to frivolity, as unexpected as a wink from a Mother Superior, is a pair of tiny loggias at the corners, each flashing a white marble pillar. Inside is a leafy patio, and the floors are decked with matting woven from dyed esparto grass, a local

Above In a land of flamboyant architecture, the renaissance palaces of Ubeda offer a soothing contrast.

Right The façade of the church of El Salvador in Ubeda, established in the sixteenth century by the secretary to the Emperor Charles V.

The bandstand in the Plaza del Primero de Mayo, Ubeda.

product which you can buy in the town's shops.

The west front of the church next door, El Salvador, makes a splendid end-piece to the square. Simple in outline – tall, with a triangular pediment and an offset tower – it is florid in detail, and would be more so had it not lost a few statues in the Civil War. The tall drums at the corners, topped with urns like samovars, the full-length buttresses, the paired renaissance pillars that flank the door and the bas-relief above it, all glow in the evening sun as though lit from within. The church was built in the mid sixteenth century by

Vandelvira from the plans of the plateresque designer Diego de Siloé, a pairing of the two greatest names in the architecture of eastern Andalusia.

After the grandeur of the façade, the interior of El Salvador comes as something of a shock. The building has a truncated look, with a tall, almost square nave leading directly into the chancel; and the warm coherence of the exterior sandstone has been exchanged for white walls and vaulting with a welter of gilt decoration, mostly from the eighteenth century. A high screen of 1557 separates nave and chancel, and there is further elaboration in the sacristy, where the roof-supports are carried by human figures carved by a Frenchman in the Italian style, an international venture of dubious success.

Behind El Salvador is the sixteenth-century Hospital de los Viejos, also by Vandelvira. Now a school, it has a fine plateresque south door and a two-sided cloister, with two tiers of arcading on round arches. A finer patio can be found inside the Palacio de las Cadenas, now the town hall: another masterpiece by Vandelvira, it is the last building on the right at the far end of the square. After the exuberance of San Salvador, its sober renaissance façade is particularly restful, taller than the parador's, with a row of oval windows on the upper storey, patrolled by a rank of statues.

Opposite it across the broad part of the square is the church of Santa Maria. The façade is simply a tall blank wall, with filled-in gothic windows, and classical pillars and pilasters continuing up into a pair of belfries. But the interior is an interesting hotch-potch. As you might guess from its dedication to the Virgin, this was once the main church in Ubeda, built on the site of a mosque inside the former castle – hence the forbidding façade. The caretaker, whose door is on the left-hand side, will show you into a gothic cloister, cramped and gloomy but with finely carved supports to the vaulting and a romanesque doorway which was once the only entrance through the castle wall. This cloister was previously the patio of the mosque, and the blank fourth wall is Moorish. Pass through it and you are in the fifteenth-century church, with severe square piers and heavy arches. When I last saw it, the seventeenth-century ceiling was *en obras*, the gallingly common phrase for 'under repairs': perhaps a signal that the wooden roof which preceded the current vaulting is being restored.

Next to Santa Maria is the former bishop's prison, beyond which are another palace and, on the corner, the former city grain store. A couple of blocks away to the north, past the left-hand end of the parador, is the main town square, the Plaza del Primero de Mayo, Mayday Square. On its left-hand corner is the old town hall, dating from 1680, with two tiers of arcading, the upper of which gave the dignitaries a good view of the bullfights which then took place here. There is another bull-viewing platform to the left of the big south door of San Pablo, whose gothic flank fills the far end of the square. The rest of the plaza is lined with handsome old houses which, though individually unassuming, cohere in a satisfying whole. The round-topped windows look out over a peaceful expanse of scattered trees, a band-stand, and a renaissance fountain of 1559. The only ugliness is a statue of St John of the Cross, and he is easily avoided.

The best feature inside San Pablo is the easternmost window on the south side, framed in elaborate gothic foliage amongst which figures lurk. On the same wall is a side chapel with a plateresque entrance of 1536, stretching from floor to ceiling. Elsewhere there are a 1380 apse, a renaissance south window and chapel screen, and a ceiling of 1763. This sounds like a mish-mash, but San Pablo is my favourite church in Ubeda. When I last went there, a nursery-school group were singing timidly to their priest; around and above them the sudden details of stonework stood out from the encircling gloom in the rare shafts of light from the narrow windows.

Of Ubeda's many remaining palaces, the best is half a kilometre west from the parador. This is the sixteenth-century house of Las Torres, named after the uncompromisingly plain square towers on either side. Between them, the short façade has been seized upon by a violent outbreak of platerism. Barely evident at the base, where the huge blank blocks of a renaissance door have kept it at bay apart from a few scallop-shell pimples, it spreads contagiously upwards until the top storey is a continuous rash of every device the mason's chisel could contrive . . . pilasters and medallions . . . wild men and angels . . . devils and dragons. The street outside is just broad enough, for once, to permit an easy view of all these fantastical details, before entering to enjoy a more restrained pleasure. Inside is an elegant renaissance patio, where the only discord-ant note is struck by the gothic gargoyles that loom above the sober medallions of the upper storey, like gate-crashers at a garden-party. Elsewhere in the palace (now a school) is a hidden chamber, only rediscovered in 1930, where a lady, clad in finery of the late sixteenth century, had been walled-in. The daughter-in-law of the palace's builder disappeared mysteriously, and this corpse may have been hers.

It is a short stroll from this palace to the southern

Above The church of San Pablo in Ubeda. Between the doors stands the saint with his sword and book, and above him is a Coronation of the Virgin.

Right Most of Ubeda's church of San Pablo post-dates 1368, when it was burnt during the civil war between Pedro the Cruel and his half-brother.

gate of the city, the Puerta de Granada. It is tiny and plain, a mere opening in one of the surviving stretches of curtain wall: yet it was through this narrow exit that Queen Isabella, on her way from Jaen, rode out to join the war against the Moors, in the final campaign that toppled the Kingdom of Granada.

The great Hospital of Santiago requires a longer detour, since it lies at the beginning of the road to Baeza, a little way west of the Plaza de Andalucia. The façade fronting the street is another variant on Vandelvira's familiar theme – a long expanse of honey-coloured stone, like the parador, but even plainer, with the wide-spaced windows shrunk almost to slits. This military severity, relieved only by an upper frieze of dark blue plaques, is accentuated by the massive towers at the corners and the huge stones that frame the doorway, beneath the mounted figure of Santiago the Moor-slayer. Inside is another of Ubeda's magnificent patios, which lack the flowers and domestic charm of the courtyards in Seville and Granada, but offer instead an aristocratic dignity and the beauty of perfect proportion. This one is large and plain, and dominated by two bulky towers flanking the church. The staircase on the right-hand side is still more grandiose, with *trompe l'oeil* frescoes decorating the walls and lofty ceiling. Very fancy, you may think, for a hospital and, since the patients were suffering from syphilis, you may also find the dedication over the front door a little inappropriate: *Maria sin pecado concebida*, Mary conceived without sin.

Baeza lies 9 kilometres away to the west. North of it, on the road to Linares and Cordoba, is the castle of Canena, but it is privately owned and can only be visited one afternoon a week. Unlike Sabiote it is in immaculate repair, and has an unexpected interior: its walls and towers are sternly military, but when you walk through the baronial entrance hall, festooned with stags' antlers like a Scottish hunting-lodge, you find yourself in a patio as fine as any in Ubeda. This dates from the sixteenth century, and is notable for the

heavily ornamented capitals of the upper-storey columns, surmounted by a frieze with blue disks similar to those on the façade of the Ubeda hospital. From the lower level a door leads out onto an exterior parapet, with a little garden and a view over the town and countryside.

But most travellers will drive straight from Ubeda to Baeza, another architectural feast. Its site is ancient, dating from the Bronze Age, and was the scene of much fighting during the Moorish period – both external and internal. Isabella razed its castle in 1476, showing that she was more afraid of her own nobles than of the Moors; but later, during the campaign of the Reconquest, the city earned the patriotic title of *El Nido Real de Gavilanes*, the Royal Nest of Falcons, in acknowledgement of its warriors' prowess against the common enemy.

Baeza is another walker's town, intimate in scale and with pleasures to the eye on almost every street. The main square is the Plaza del Mercado, with the arcaded corn exchange on the east side, a reminder of the fertility of the surrounding countryside. But there are better sights in the small adjoining square to the south, the Plaza del Populo. In its centre is the Lion Fountain, said to have been brought here from the Carthaginian (and Roman) city of Castulo. The four slavering beasts around the base raise the possibility that the figure in the middle is Cybele, an earth-goddess often depicted with lions in attendance: but local tradition maintains that she is Hannibal's wife Himilce. Unfortunately, during the Civil War she was taken to be neither of these ladies, but the Virgin Mary, and her head was chopped off. Since then she has sprouted a new one.

At one corner of the square is the Jaen arch, once part of the city walls. Its little balcony is reputedly original, and the first Mass was said here after the town's recapture from the Moors. Adjoining the gate on one side is a larger arch added in 1521, and on the other is the Casa del Populo, an early sixteenth-century stone building with elaborate upper-storey windows in the plateresque style. Next to it again is the world's most handsome slaughterhouse, now a museum: its pilastered upper gallery, the decorative frieze and Charles V's huge coat of arms all suggest that

The rich plains around Ubeda produce two of the peasant staples, bread and olive oil.

171

butchers were a more aesthetic breed in the sixteenth century.

A flight of steps to the left of the Casa del Populo leads to the Cuesta de San Gil, from which you can bear left to reach the Plaza de Santa Maria. Here the seminary of San Felipe Neri of 1660 is on the left, and in the middle of the square is an unusual fountain of 1564, incorporating a triumphal arch. On the right, adjoining the handsome gothic Palace of Los Cabrera, is the sombre north façade of the cathedral. It looks like a much-patched tapestry of grey and gold stone, with in-filled windows and little detailing. This disordered appearance reflects a chequered history. Originally a mosque, the first Christian church was inaugurated by Alfonso VII in 1147 and expanded by St Ferdinand: but it fell down, and was replaced in the sixteenth century by the present building, partly the work of Vandelvira. Some relics of its earlier life survive, including the lower courses of the tower, formerly the minaret of the mosque, and the fine Moorish west door next to it, the Puerta de la Luna, Gateway of the Moon.

After the austere exterior, the cathedral's interior is a surprise. It is tall and light, with clustered pale stone columns. There is an interesting little cloister, massively gothic with Moorish-style side-chapels on the south side, a 1580 pulpit in coloured iron, and two sixteenth-century screens by the iron-master Bartolomé. The punitively baroque main altarpiece is best avoided, but the church can offer a special party-trick at the west end: slip a coin into a slot, and a panel in the wall slides back, as in a horror-film, to reveal a 2-metre tall reliquary dating from 1714. Celestial music plays and the ornate monstrosity slowly revolves, before vanishing again from sight.

A stroll down the Calle San Juan Bautista, to the right on leaving the cathedral, leads to an esplanade that runs along the city walls, with a broad vista of the cornfields in the Guadalquivir valley. Or you can head back into the city centre via the Cuesta de San Felipe,

The triumphal arch and fountain in the cathedral square at Baeza. Behind it is the seminary of San Felipe Neri.

opposite the cathedral entrance. This route passes the most spectacular of Baeza's palaces, the Palace of Jabalquinto. The façade is truly amazing. Like the Casa de las Torres in Ubeda it has a pustular look, thanks to the stone bosses that stud the wall. The door and windows are in the Isabelline gothic style of the late fifteenth century, characterized by ogee arches framed in elaborate decoration. What little space remains is filled with pinnacles, pine-cones and heraldic shields. This confection is topped by an arcaded loggia and flanked by the oddest feature of all – a pair of massive rounded pilasters which erupt into capitals dripping with stalactites. This rich extravaganza offers further confirmation that the predominantly fifteenth- and sixteenth-century architecture of Ubeda and Baeza manages to cater to every taste, by alternating the sober façades of Vandelvira and his school with the eclectic exuberance of stonework such as this. And indeed the contrasts continue inside, where a renaissance patio of rare delicacy leads to a massive baroque staircase, with lions that snarl at you as you pass.

The next building is the old university, founded in 1542, when there were 32 universities in Spain. Facing it and the Jabalquinto palace is the tiny romanesque church of Santa Cruz, the only one to survive from the period of the Reconquest. It has, alas, been much restored, but it retains a Visigothic arch and some frescoes from the fifteenth and sixteenth centuries. A detour past the side of it soon leads to another of the city gates, the Puerta de Ubeda, with a portion of the ramparts and a keep attached. Or continue up the Cuesta de San Felipe back to the Plaza del Mercado.

The street to the north, the Calle San Pablo, typifies the gold-and-white beauty of Baeza, Ubeda and Jaen. In between the stretches of whitewash are the sandstone façades of a number of palaces, decked with the coats of arms of their noble founders, and with the decorative tricks inherited from the Moors – framed windows and internal patios. Although this area lay outside the old walls, times had become more peaceable when these houses were built, and in any case Isabella had pulled most of the walls down.

Opposite the best group of palaces is the church of San Pablo, its unremarkable exterior concealing a

composed and austere interior in pure gothic style. Spare a glance for some of the incidental details: the fluted font in the north-west corner, the beaked birds on the arms of the bishop's throne – the most elaborate of the stalls at the west end – and a triptych which may or may not be by Van Dyck.

The remaining sights in Baeza are to the west of the Plaza del Mercado. Conveniently, the furthest is the least rewarding. This is the church of San Andres, of which the best features are its plateresque doorway, its mid sixteenth-century choir-stalls, and nine fifteenth-century painted panels. Much nearer is the town hall, a block away from the plaza. Attributed to Vandelvira, it was once a combined law-court and jail, thereby streamlining the course of justice. It is a handsome and idiosyncratic building. The proportions, long and low, are renaissance, but the detailing is plateresque. The upper windows are so elaborate that you feel you are looking at two different façades superimposed one upon the other, fancy above and plain below, like thick icing on a dry cake. This town hall and the one in Seville – though the treatment there is different – are two of the best buildings in Andalusia for assessing your reaction to the plateresque style.

A short stroll round the corner to the north-west brings you to another creation of the industrious Vandelvira, the convent of San Francisco. But an earthquake, storms and the French (who stabled their horses here) have reduced it to a ruin; although a fine doorway survives, it is currently under scaffolding. So head south-west instead, to the church of San Salvador.

This is a romantic spot, offering a succession of styles which contribute to an air of elegant spaciousness and poetic neglect. Its modest thirteenth-century

doorway is sturdily romanesque, but the long nave and accompanying aisles have a Moorish-style roof with painted tie-beams, resting on tall plain columns. The light that floods through the makeshift windows on the north side, and the plain brick floor, give the interior an atmosphere which is, somehow, more scholastic than ecclesiastic. Outside, the reason for the bare north windows is apparent: the church has lost the roof of a further north aisle, and weeds grow among the paving-stones and the mouldering masonry of the romanesque and gothic arches. The early thirteenth-century tower has a feature which is something of a Baeza trade-mark – the coats of arms of the bishop who built it, set curiously into the very corners.

There is much more to see in Baeza, if you have the time to wander around the back streets. And then there are the processions, if you are here during one of the religious festivals. Baeza is traditionally a pious town, with more local saints than any other in Spain (and a claim to be the birthplace of the eleven thousand virgins of Cologne, though this seems to be somewhat stretching the resources of such a small place). So the Easter processions are well done, as they are at Ubeda, a passionate microcosm of the more famous celebrations in Seville (see p. 30). Many of the floats paraded by the twenty different brotherhoods are of considerable age, dating from the Seville school of the sixteenth and seventeenth centuries. There is another parade on the feast of Corpus Christi, and on 8 September, the Fiesta of the Virgin, there is a *romeria* or pilgrimage, a smaller version of the spectacle at El Rocio (see p. 33). Horsemen with women behind them in Andalusian dress, and streams of decorated carriages, process beyond the city bounds and into the surrounding fields, and play music and stage flamboyant riding contests. Here among the olive plantations and the dust, under the warm autumn sky, you may feel that little has changed, after all, during the centuries since these celebrations began.

Aceite de oliva, todo mal quita: olive oil cures every ill.

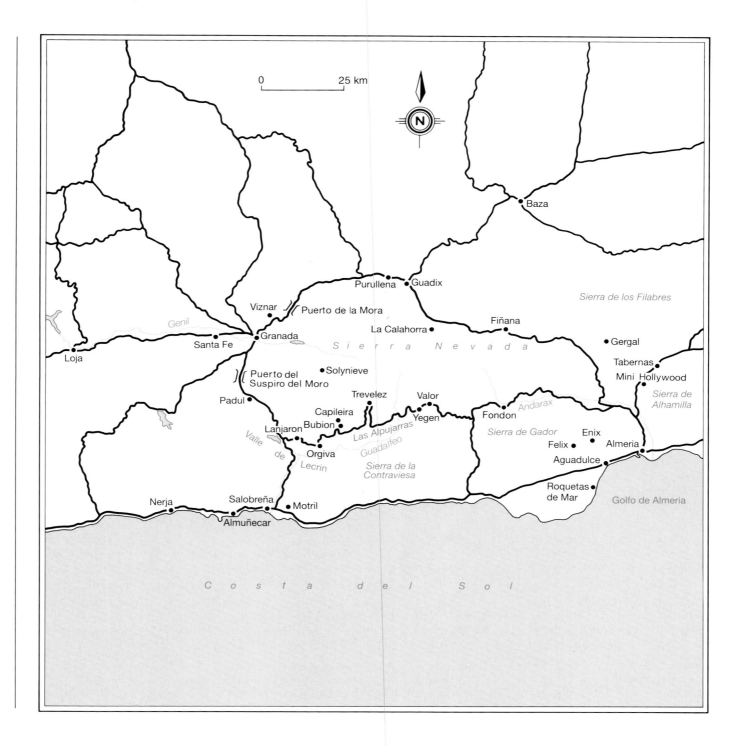

0   25 km

N

Baza

Purullena   Guadix

Sierra de los Filabres

Viznar   Puerto de la Mora

Genil

Fiñana

La Calahorra

Gergal

Granada

S i e r r a   N e v a d a

Tabernas

Santa Fe

Mini Hollywood

Loja

Solynieve

Puerto del
Suspiro del Moro

Sierra de
Alhamilla

Trevelez

Valor

Padul

Andarax

Capileira

Yegen

Fondon

Sierra de Gador

Enix

Lanjaron   Bubion

Las Alpujarras

Almeria

Valle

Guadalfeo

Felix

Orgiva

de

Aguadulce

Lecrin

Sierra de la
Contraviesa

Roquetas
de Mar

Golfo de Almeria

Nerja   Salobreña

Motril

Almuñecar

C o s t a   d e l   S o l

6
Granada and the South-East

Santa Fe – Granada – Viznar – Guadix – La Calahorra –
Mini Hollywood – Almeria – the Alpujarras – Yegen –
Trevelez – Lanjaron – Salobreña – Almuñecar

The Mores believe Granada Ly's
Directly under Paradise
And that they differ both no more
Than th'upper Roomes do from the Floure.

Samuel Butler

I saw the Alhambra in a steady
drizzle, and it seemed to me
shoddy and bedraggled, like a
gypsy girl sitting under a damp hedge.

Gerald Brenan

Seville and Cordoba both lie in the flat plain of the Guadalquivir. The third great Moorish city, Granada, is suspended on a mountain slope. Above the city, visible from very far off, are the snows of the Sierra Nevada, which linger throughout the year, lightly dusted from time to time with sand from the Sahara, like grated nutmeg on a Crême Chantilly. Below is the sweep of the Vega, the huge upland valley transformed by the Moors into a garden of over 200,000 hectares, which was filled with orchards, villas, thirty water-mills and three hundred farms. It is typical of the Moorish genius that their last capital in Spain should be a place which so combines the aesthetic and the functional.

Although there were three Roman settlements in the area of Granada, it was only in the eleventh century that the city achieved any influence. When the Cordoba-based Moorish empire broke up, Granada declared itself independent, but soon lost its freedom to Berber invaders from Morocco. These were overthrown in 1238, and Granada finally reached its apogee under the Nasrids, who moved their capital here from Jaen, when the latter was captured by St Ferdinand. The Nasrids built the Medinat al-Hamra,

now called the Alhambra, the jewel of Granada and indeed of all Andalusia.

The Nasrid empire paid annual tribute to the Christians – it even helped St Ferdinand capture Seville, and later, in the fourteenth century, Pedro the Cruel borrowed Nasrid craftsmen and architects. This equivocation enabled it to survive until the end of the fifteenth century. By this time, swollen by Muslim refugees from the rest of Spain, the population had reached 200,000, four times that of London. But for all their wealth and their far-famed cultural style, the Nasrids were little more than mountain barons, obsessed with their own tribal squabbles (there were fourteen changes of sultanship between 1417–64). Whereas Cordoba in its heyday looked out across the whole of Europe, Granada looked inwards, to its walled gardens and colonnaded courts and blood-stained knives. It is significant that the Alhambra is not merely one of the world's most decorative palaces, but also one of the most intimate.

Just as the cause of the Moorish invasion has been attributed to a slighted woman – the daughter of a North African governor, seduced by the last king of Visigothic Spain – so the Moors' final demise was

GRANADA AND THE SOUTH-EAST

inaugurated by another. The Sultan Muley Hassan abandoned his queen Ayesha for a Christian captive, known to the Moors as Zoraya. Factions formed around the two women. In 1482 Hassan was deposed by Ayesha's son, Boabdil, *El Rey Chico*, the Boy King, who became the last monarch of Granada. This sundering of the city's strength came precisely when Christian Spain was being united by the alliance of Castile and Aragon through the marriage of Ferdinand and Isabella. The luckless Boabdil – one of life's born losers – was twice captured by Ferdinand, but was cunningly released to further the dynastic squabbling which was wracking Granada in his absence. In 1492 it was he who handed over the city's keys to the Catholic monarchs, and departed weeping to the wilderness of the south.

The place where Boabdil's surrender was signed lies just off the N342 to the west. Eleven kilometres short of the city, with the Alhambra already visible on its hill and the Sierra Nevada suspended in the sky behind it, the road bypasses the small, shabby town of Santa Fe. It is square, and quartered by two main roads meeting in a central plaza – a Roman ground-plan. But as the chapels over the four gates suggest, Santa Fe was not built by the Romans. This was the site of the Christian camp during the final siege of Granada, a silken city of gay pavilions, awnings and banners. The largest and most splendid tent was Isabella's: but while she was at her prayers she left a candle burning too near her brocade hangings. A gust of wind, and the tent was alight, and with it the whole camp. The Moors, suspecting a stratagem, failed to take advantage: but Isabella was determined to avoid a repetition, and also to signal that she was there to stay. She ordered the construction of a permanent town, and it was completed in eighty days, with the men of nine Spanish cities vying in its construction. To the Moorish patrols, the clang of each mason's hammer was the knell of doom.

High on the west façade of the church which was

The Sierra Nevada, the highest mountains in Europe south of the Alps.

later built in the central square is a curious device – a lance and a strip of parchment, resting on a turbaned head. It celebrates two connected incidents among the many tales of personal daring and individual combat that enlivened the slow months of the siege. First, a Christian knight led a small band into Granada under cover of darkness, and affixed a sign bearing an *Ave Maria* to the main door of the chief mosque. In retaliation, a Moorish knight, a famous giant of a warrior, rode his horse in front of the Christian camp with the *Ave Maria* attached to its tail. The two knights met in single combat. The Christian won, and it is the giant's head, together with the victor's lance and the *Ave Maria*, which are still displayed in Santa Fe. Another plaque on the same church claims that this square also saw the signing of Columbus's commission to sail to the Indies. Much history for so small a place. Nowadays its main flurry of activity is during the festival of St Augustine on 28 August, when giants and huge-headed figures parade the streets, and there is a pilgrimage of carts and riders to the shrine of the saint.

As you enter Granada, the old town disappears behind the long cliff of high-rise buildings which have sprung up to the west, along the bottom of the three ridges which jut from the foothills of the sierra. The right-hand ridge contains little of interest except some outlying fortifications. The centre ridge, across the green cleft of the Darro valley, is crowned with the russet towers of the Alhambra, while the left-hand ridge holds the steep warren of the Albaicin, the oldest part of the city and the original seat of government. The way to the Alhambra rises from the central Plaza Nueva, up the narrow Cuesta de Gomeres. This passes through a sixteenth-century gateway, and into a forest of elms and oaks and black poplars, traditionally planted by the Duke of Wellington in the early nineteenth century. After a few hundred metres you can park your car at a road junction beside the Hotel Washington Irving. Irving, the American writer and ambassador to Spain from 1842–6, stayed for a while in the Alhambra, and his *Conquest of Granada* makes vivid holiday reading.

Looming above are the walls of the citadel. Turn left when you reach them, and walk up alongside the

ramparts. Punctuated by towers old and new, they ring the entire hilltop and enclose the buildings that survive – the original castle, predating the Nasrids, which sits at the point of the ridge, the Alhambra palace itself, and next to it the later renaissance palace of the Emperor Charles V. Further along the ridge are a church, a monastery converted into a parador, and the motley relics of the town that once filled the remaining space within the fortifications.

Pass the first side-turning, and continue a further 250 metres to the Gate of Justice, named after the area outside, which was once used for civil courts and occasional executions. Dating from 1348, its exterior face carries a wryly cross-denominational collection of signs: a hand to protect against the Evil Eye, a key symbolizing power, and inside the arch a Virgin and Child. She looks as uneasy amid the surrounding *sebka* work as she did among the bright tiles of Pilate's House in Seville.

From the inner gate, which still retains its Moorish doors, a flight of steps leads up to the top of the hill, and to the oldest gate of all, the Wine Gate, now semi-detached but once part of an inner defensive wall. Dating from the thirteenth century, it is more delicate than the rest of the military masonry, and exquisitely decorated, with keyhole arches surrounded with tiles and surmounted with double windows. The tilework has an Indian look, a reflection of the extent of the Muslim empire at that time. The gate's name may be a corruption of Arabic spelling, or the building may once have been used as a wine-store – post-Conquest, of course, since the Moors were forbidden to drink the stuff.

But what dominates the immediate scene is the palace of Charles V, the Holy Roman Emperor who succeeded Ferdinand of Aragon as King of Spain (where, confusingly, he was Charles I). The surest way to infuriate your more aesthetic friends is to say that this is the best part of the Alhambra. A more tactful

A bronze hitching ring in the Florentine style, in the palace of Charles V in the Alhambra.

judgment, often made, is that it would have been better built elsewhere. It is without doubt a handsome building in the Italian renaissance style – according to some pundits the finest in Spain. But to most eyes its sheer size and its aggressive styling, with rough-hewn blocks and great bronze rings hanging from the mouths of lions and eagles, give it the arrogance of a conqueror's jack-boot implanted in the heart of the victim's citadel.

It was begun in 1526, because Charles had found the Alhambra palace too uncomfortable on his occasional visits to Granada: but cash soon ran out, and the construction was abandoned several times. The final ring of roof-tiles was only added recently. They are the only Spanish feature about the building, apart from the circular inner court, which looks more like a bull-ring than a palace. And indeed it was used for bull-fighting – there are bulls' heads in the Doric frieze

Quien no ha visto Granada, no ha visto nada: he who has not seen Granada has seen nothing. The view of the Alhambra from the Albaicin.

between the two galleries which surround it.

The ground floor contains the National Museum of Hispano-Muslim Art, a collection of carvings, pottery and glassware mostly assembled from the Alhambra. Two exhibits stand out: a fourteenth- or fifteenth-century urn in faded golds and blues, somewhat battered but still the finest surviving specimen of its kind; and a tenth-century marble ablution bowl showing four lions devouring four stags, with predators and victims so formally disposed as to resemble a ballet, a dance of death.

Upstairs is the Fine Arts Museum, where the collection of Granadine paintings is eclipsed by a handful of unusually fine sculptures by Montañés, Cano (the seventeenth-century architect and painter), Siloé and Jacobo Florentino (both better known as sixteenth-century architects). Look out too for the triptych of the Gran Capitan (see p.197), a masterpiece of Limoges enamel from c.1500: in the panel showing the Last Judgement, there is a touch of wit – two priests, one among the saved and one among the damned.

Opposite the main door of the palace loom the walls of the *alcazaba*, the earliest fortified site on the hill, predating the Alhambra palace. The open space before it was once a dry moat, subsequently converted by the Christians to a huge underground cistern. Inside the castle is a wide courtyard, the Plaza de Armas, with some well-like apertures leading down into broad caverns below. Originally storage cisterns, these were later used as dungeons into which Christian slaves were lowered at night, and hauled out again at dawn for their labour under the lash. The other end of the plaza is filled with the foundations of the Moorish houses which once covered the area.

At the far left corner is an exit which leads on to a battlement walk, planted with a narrow garden which is usually deserted. There are palms and cypresses inside necklaces of fragrant box hedges, lilies, two

curiously carved fountains, and a tall bower of wisteria. The stone benches are not conducive to prolonged meditation, but you can hardly fault their situation. Sitting here at peace, looking across the bright green grove below to the snows of the mountains beyond, you can imagine yourself a Nasrid king. The beauty of the scene has its own epigraph, too; a plaque on the tower on your right as you enter the garden, the Torre de Polvora, reads:

> Dale limosna, mujer,
> Que no hay en la vida nada
> Como la pena de ser
> ciego en Granada.
> (Give freely, for no fate is harder
> Than to be blind – and in Granada.)

The view is even better from the top of the Torre de la Vela or watch-tower, the highest tower of the *alcazaba*. On one side, on a parallel ridge across the little valley of the Darro, is the Albaicin district, the oldest part of Granada and the seat of government before the Nasrids built the Alhambra. Its hillside is covered with a froth of white houses, interrupted by the patios of two or three palaces, which are now convents. Between the houses, cypresses and patches of green signal the *carmenes*, the hanging gardens which are so secretly enclosed that only from here can you appreciate their number. Church-towers crown the ridge, and to the right a long slope rises to the Sacromonte, with its gypsy caves.

Ahead of you, to the left of the Albaicin, is the long vista of the Vega, fringed on every side by mountains, blue in the haze. The sluices of the irrigation channels that still criss-cross it are regulated by the bell on the tower beside you. Richard Ford claimed that in still weather it could be heard in Loja, 50 kilometres away. It is also rung on 7 and 8 October to commemorate the Battle of Lepanto in 1571, when the Ottoman Turks were flung back from the western Mediterranean: and on 2 January, that most significant of all Granada's dates, when it was surrendered to the Christians in 1492. To the left the view continues, across a leafy valley to the Torres Bermejas, an extension of the Alhambra's fortifications, and up to the Sierra Nevada.

The courtyard of Charles V's palace in the Alhambra is curved like a bull-ring, and was formerly used as such.

183

Behind you can be seen the layout of the Alhambra itself, albeit somewhat obscured by Charles V's great cube. On one side is the palace, with some curtain towers beyond it, which continue out of sight to enclose the whole ridge. Outside this circuit is the garden of the Generalife, on a higher shoulder of hill to the left, at the top of which are some more fortifications, the Silla del Moro. Across the threadbare little Patio de Machuca is the entrance to the Alhambra palace, one of the world's great works of art. It is as well to be prepared for what you will see.

First, anyone expecting size and grandeur is in for a shock. Instead of vast marble halls, the visitor is faced with the intricacy of a jewelled watch. The Moors were miniaturists and, in their domestic arrangements, reclusive. The palace is enclosed and intimate: but what it lacks in scale it gains in detail. In its day, almost every centimetre of wall and ceiling was decorated.

This decoration is different from most other Arabic work in Andalusia, not because of its age – Pedro's palace in Seville is roughly contemporary – but because it was made by Moors for Moors (as was Cordoba's mosque), not by Christians in the Moorish style. Most of what you see today was built during two successive phases, the first under Yusuf I in the mid fourteenth century, and the second towards the end of the century by Mohammed V. Much is restored: but the real marvel is that so much should have survived at all. After the Reconquest the palace was variously used as an asylum for debtors and invalid soldiers, a prison for convicts and galley-slaves, a silk factory, a powder magazine, a salt-fish store and a pen for donkeys and sheep.

Its most dedicated despoilers were often its custodians, who tore off door locks and tiles for sale, and sawed up the carved woodwork. Trees grew in the patios, and their roots invaded the intricate pipework of the fountains. There was a gunpowder explosion in 1591, and sundry earthquakes. An 1833 water-colour by an English visitor shows artisans living and working in one of the towers, with baulks of timber propped against the delicate plasterwork, and buckets hanging among the fretted stalactites: and an engraving by Gustave Doré, a generation later, shows a tourist, hammer in hand, about to dislodge a tile as a souvenir, while his wife, cloaked and conspiratorial, at least has the grace to look over her shoulder with a semblance of guilt.

The heart of Yusuf's palace is the Court of the Myrtles, where the visitor comes face to face with Moorish architecture at its greatest. The long side walls are simple, though each little *sebka*-decked window is a delight. The riches lie at the ends, where sheets of *sebka*, the colour of old ivory, flow down the walls like finely-woven fabric to meet the brilliantly tiled dadoes below. Down the middle, between the myrtle hedges, is a long pool. From the south end the view is of the Comares Tower, whose blank brickwork and arrogant merlons contrast with the delicacy of the arcade beneath: power and luxury conjoined. In the water, barely rippled at each end by a pair of simple fountains, the slim arches are reflected. Within the central arch, shining in the darkness beyond it, is a pair of windows.

The base of the tower is filled by the Hall of the Ambassadors, and in front of those central windows is where the Sultan once sat upon his throne. From here, by barely moving his head, he could regale his senses with the delights of water, earth and air. Ahead is the shining ribbon of the patio's pool. On either side the deep bayed windows look out over the vast panorama of hill and valley. And above is a dome, 25 metres high, of cypress-wood inlaid with mother-of-pearl, in starry patterns portraying the seven Islamic heavens. Stretching from ceiling to dado, and out into the bays of the windows (where it can be studied most easily), is a display of *sebka* work which is simply stunning, an endless succession of friezes and panels decorated with sunburst patterns and foliate designs, alternating with poems and aphorisms in two kinds of Arabic script. Amongst these is the oft-repeated invocation 'There is no conqueror but Allah', the words of Mohammed I (1238–72), the first Nasrid king, when he returned

Plasterwork in the Alhambra. The Muslim religion permitted the use of foliage and flowers, but not of animals or humans.

from helping his religious enemies, the Christians, to capture Seville. The most-quoted judgment on this extraordinary room was that of Charles V: 'Ill-fated was the man who lost all this.'

The newer half of the palace is also centred on a masterpiece. The Patio of the Lions, begun in 1377, is different from the others in that it is surrounded by arcading on all four sides, like the palace patios in Seville and Cordoba. And it has two inspirations that are all its own: the pavilions that jut into the courtyard from either end, each with its own fountain: and the main fountain in the centre, resting on the backs of twelve much eroded lions, spouting water from their blunt muzzles. To the acerbic Ford, 'their faces are barbecued, their manes cut like the scales of a griffin, and the legs like bed-posts', but their plain weightiness contrasts wonderfully with the elaboration around them.

Alexandre Dumas described this patio as a dream turned to stone by a magician's wand, and its detailing represents the final achievement of Moorish art in Spain. It is for you to decide whether the style is an apogee, or the beginning of decadence. Is the *sebka*-work quite as exquisite as that in the Hall of the Ambassadors? And those arches, so deep that they are two-thirds the height of the supporting columns, are they perhaps over-exaggerated? As for the ceilings, the test case is in the Sala de los Abencerrajes, where Boabdil is alleged to have conducted a small massacre: your guide will conjure up bloodstains in the fountain – but to me the oozing stalactites overhead are far more sinister.

There is a more satisfying room opposite – the Sala de los Dos Hermanas. The ceiling here is an illustration of how miraculous it is that the Alhambra has survived: it contains nearly 5000 separate pieces, made from nothing stronger than plaster, strengthened here and there with pieces of reed. Beyond is an arch leading to an outer room, off which is the wonderful little Mirador de Daraxa, which looks down into the garden below, and formerly out over the vista beyond – until Charles V built his apartments in the way.

The route to these apartments passes the royal baths, a multi-coloured version of the simple brick constructions seen elsewhere. The tiles are mostly eighteenth-century, the floors are marble, and there is an arcade at each end. Next door is a cooling-off room, the Sala de Camas, where the coloured tiles have taken over with a vengeance, and prolonged lolling in one of the deep recesses would have risked severe eye-strain. Above, surrounded by a welter of coloured stucco, is a gallery from which the Sultan could inspect the bathers. According to one tradition, he would throw an apple to the woman he selected for the night.

On the outer wall nearby, an exterior gallery with daintily painted beams and ceiling leads to the Tocador de la Reina, a delightful bird-cage propped on a tower, with magnificent views and sixteenth-century frescoes. This was built by Charles V as a dressing-room for his wife, and next door are his own apartments, where the linen-fold panelling comes as a culture-shock after all the *sebka*-work. Charles himself never stayed here, but Washington Irving did. He wrote to a friend: 'I have never had such a delicious abode. One of my windows looks into the little garden of Lindaraxa; the citron trees are full of blossom and perfume the air. . . .' He also swam in the pool of the Court of the Myrtles, while an elderly count shot at swallows from the balconies.

The Partal Gardens outside the Alhambra are newer than the palace. The pleasantly haphazard array of terraces, scented with roses and box hedges, reflects the fact that this area was once covered by palaces occupied by the nobles, officials and concubines of the court. Part of one of these survives – the Torre de las Damas, with its pool in front of it, presided over by a brace of lions. On the left of the tower are the only relics of the humbler Moorish dwellings which not merely housed the palace's servants, but formed a sizeable town – the *poblacion* – that once filled the bailey within the Alhambra's walls.

At this end of the hill, the defences are only intact on one side. The towers to the south were blown up by the French when they retreated in the Peninsular War.

'A dream turned to stone by a magician's wand': the Patio of the Lions in the Alhambra palace, Granada.

All the other towers would have gone too, had it not been for one Jose Garcia, who cut the fuse that had been laid around the walls, according to a plaque near the Wine Tower.

The biggest of these sadly truncated towers, the Torre de los Siete Suelos or Tower of the Seven Storeys, was once the main entrance to the Alhambra, and held the gateway through which Boabdil is said to have left his palace for the last time. He asked for it to be walled up afterwards, and it is certainly well blocked now, by an eighteenth-century gun emplacement. The tower also held a ghost, doubtless exorcised by the French explosion, which guarded the Sultan's treasure, and toured Granada at night disguised as a headless horse followed by six hounds.

Outside the Alhambra, on a higher hillside across a small ravine, stands the Generalife, the rural refuge of the Nasrid kings. The only significant buildings are two pavilions, and these are much restored: but their basic structure is older than the surviving Alhambra palace, and between them lies a precious example of a Moorish garden. It is based on the most ancient ground-plan in the civilized world. Roman villas had enclosed gardens, with a central pool surrounded by cool colonnaded walks decorated with mosaics, as at Italica and Bruñel (*see* pp. 32 and 154). But the layout is much older than the Romans: the cities of Mesopotamia in 3000 BC were also composed of houses built around an inner court. Much later, monasteries and university colleges in northern Europe adopted the same plan.

The Generalife is reached from a carpark along the ridge or from a gate at the far end of the Alhambra, through gardens of parterres and oleanders. The façade of the first pavilion is plain and crumbling, deluged with wisteria. Below it is the former entrance, once connected with the Alhambra by the Nasrids' private bridge: and inside is the main garden, the Patio de la Acequia. Down its centre runs a pool, pointing a long, narrow finger at the arches and loggia of the pavilion beyond, and lined with a double row of fountains that lean lazily inwards. Within the shabby side-walls are flowerbeds, earthenware pots, and a few trees. The elements are simple and much of the masonry is plain: yet viewing the scene through the narrow entrance arch, drugged by the flicker of the fountains and the scent of blossom, the visitor has no doubt that he is looking at one of the great gardens of the world.

There are dramatic vistas over the Alhambra and the Albaicin from a mirador on the left-hand side and from the pavilion at the far end, both of which retain elements of the original Moorish decoration. From the latter, signs direct you up to the Patio de los Cipreses where Boabdil, showing more acumen than usual, is said to have surprised his wife with a lover, their ears perhaps dulled by the murmur of the fountains. The lover was an Abencerraje, which is said to have prompted the massacre in the Lion Court. Higher still is a nineteenth-century belvedere, from which you can return via a cascade staircase, where rivulets of water stream down the banisters on either side. At the top of the hill is the Moor's Seat, where the castle and cisterns are currently under restoration.

Compared with the Alhambra, Granada's main Christian monument, the cathedral, lies well concealed, masked by the surrounding buildings. Originally gothic at its inception in 1521, its style was soon hijacked by the renaissance architect Diego de Siloé, who also had a hand in the cathedrals of Cadiz, Seville, Guadix and Malaga and several other Andalusian churches. After his death in 1563 the work continued, and the massive west front was not finally completed until 1714. The interior is light and well-proportioned, with clustered pillars supporting simple vaults. It is the details which are sumptuous, notably the doors leading to the Capilla Real and the sanctuary, the double organ (1750) and pulpits, the chapels round the perimeter, and the statuary from different periods and of varying merit. At the entrance to Siloé's loftily domed Capilla Mayor is a quizzically linked pairing of sculptures high on the walls – Ferdinand and Isabella surmounted by Adam and Eve, the latter two by Alonso Cano. Born in 1601, he was a versatile fellow

---

Fountains playing in the Patio de la Acequia in Granada's Generalife, the royal gardens outside the Alhambra palace.

who also designed the west façade, executed a number of the cathedral's canvases and carvings, fled to Madrid after fighting a duel, survived a trial for the murder of his wife (he claimed that as an artist his right hand should be spared from torture), and eventually became a canon of the cathedral. His sculptures are wonderfully restrained for the period, notably a dainty blue-and-green *Immaculate Conception* in the sanctuary.

Adjoining the cathedral is the smaller but more rewarding Capilla Real. Begun in 1506 as a mausoleum for Ferdinand and Isabella, it is a compact and unified example of, appropriately, the Isabelline gothic style, with its double-bend arches and elaborate detailing. The huge wrought-iron screen (1520) by Bartolomé of Jaen, which fences off the chancel, is the finest in Spain, which means – in this style – in the world. The predominating colours are gold and black, the main figures are cast in the half-round, and the wealth of detail suggests the transference of plateresque stone-work to mid-air. As with some of Andalusia's palace façades, the elaboration proliferates as it develops upwards, progressing from plain columns through a stratum of royal coats of arms, signatures, and yoke-and-arrow motifs (the emblem of Ferdinand and Isabella), up to a splendid frieze depicting the life of Christ.

Inside the chancel lie the Catholic monarchs themselves, somewhat eclipsed by the screen, and by the presence next to them, on a higher plinth, of their daughter Joan the Mad and her husband Philip the Fair. On either side of the reredos are the monarchs again, kneeling, in what are said to be accurate portraits by Siloé. The warrior queen looks slightly podgy, as she does on her tomb, and her hands are apart as though clapping. Certainly history owes her some applause. Devout, determined, brave, the great-granddaughter of John of Gaunt and mother-in-law (through his first queen) of Henry VIII, she changed the history of Spain and hence of Europe. Ferdinand

---

The sculptural details in the cathedral at Granada are often more satisfying than the overall design.

was no slouch either. Soldier, politician and occasional philanderer, he eventually controlled the whole of Spain and used diplomacy or the sword to win territory in France, Italy and Africa.

The monarchs' actual remains lie in lead coffins below the chancel, with a candle burning perpetually before Isabella, as she had ordained. The vault is tiny – a small room, as Charles V remarked, for so great a glory. Shakespeare said much the same of another place: 'Glories, triumphs, spoils, shrunk to this little measure!'

Some of Isabella's glories are next door in the sacristy – a magnificent collection of fifteenth-century Dutch paintings. Van der Weyden shows Christ as a shrivelled foetus in his *Nativity*, and again after death in a *Pieta*, where his arms swing out at right-angles to echo the crucifixion. There is also a fine triptych of the Passion by Dieric Bouts, and half a dozen masterpieces by Hans Memling. Isabella's crown and sceptre are there too, and Ferdinand's sword, and the queen's mirror converted to a custodial, piously combining vanity with spirituality.

Opposite the entrances to the cathedral and Capilla Real is the old town hall, once a fourteenth-century religious school attached to the city's mosque, which formerly stood on the site of the sanctuary. Between its elaborate rococo windows the walls are strangely painted to resemble marble, although the purple blobs are more suggestive of plum-pudding. The alleys to the right are narrow, since they reflect the ground-plan of the old Moorish city, and they lead to the *alcaicería*, the former silk market. The original bazaar here was destroyed by fire in 1843, but it has been imaginatively reconstructed, with horseshoe arches to the 200 stalls, and cobbled passageways that intersect every few metres. Bright bolts of cloth dangle enticingly before your eyes, together with leatherwork and the products of other local crafts, offering both the visual delights and the financial temptations of an oriental *souk*.

A hundred and fifty metres away, across the main Calle de los Reyes Catolicos, is a building that is genuinely old. This is the Casa del Carbon, the only complete example in Spain of a Middle-Eastern inn or

Above The façade of the Capilla Real in Granada, commissioned by Isabella as her mausoleum two months before her death, but only completed thirteen years later.

Right The *alcaicería*, or silk market, in Granada. The Arabic word is said to derive from 'Caesar', reputedly the Emperor Justinian who conferred silk-weaving rights on the Arabs.

caravanserai (though there are the partial remains of a smaller one in Cordoba). It is built around a courtyard which is entered through an entrance elaborate enough to convey that this was a five-star establishment. The yard still has a watering-trough in the centre, and is surrounded by three bleakly simple tiers of galleries, the lowest for the merchants' animals and goods, and the upper two for their own accommodation. After the Reconquest the building became a home for charcoal-burners – hence its name – and later a theatre. Today it stands empty and silent; but this 650-year-old monument to the muleteer's trade is more evocative than many of those devoted to power or wealth or religion.

Half a kilometre to the north is the beginning of the Albaicin, the oldest inhabited sector of Granada. Climbing up the steep hill on which it is built is strenuous, but a fair idea of its character can be gained by walking along the level street at the bottom, the Carrera del Darro, which leads out of the Plaza Nueva. On the left side of the Plaza is the Audiencia of 1531, and at the far end is the elegant little church of Santa Ana, designed by Siloé, with a plateresque doorway and a slender tower flecked with coloured tiles. Beyond it, between the twin hills of the Albaicin and the Alhambra, the Carrera del Darro runs past the miniature jungle that fills the narrow valley of the River Darro: huge fig trees burgeon beside the snow-fed stream, two high-arched bridges cross it (the second dating originally from the eleventh century), and the towers of the Alhambra are silhouetted against the sky on the right.

Almost every building here is of interest. Opposite the church is the Casa de los Pisas, where San Juan de Dios died in 1550. This itinerant saint, a bookseller, was born in Portugal and fought the Turks as far afield as Hungary, but finally settled in Granada. A little further, at no. 37, are my favourite Arab baths. Their entrance leads into a tiny patio with black-and-white cobbles and a central pool, and thence to a vaulted room of bare brick where the bathers left their clothes. The characteristic star-shaped and octagonal vents in the ceiling were once filled with coloured glass, which must have scattered vivid patterns on the floor. Next is a larger room with a couple of Moorish arches at one end, where the clients rested and chatted on couches. Finally, you enter the main bath-room, splendidly colonnaded on three sides with horseshoe arches resting on columns topped with a variety of capitals brought from Cordoba: two are Roman, a couple are Visigothic and some are caliphal. Beyond is the hot-room, where the fire for the underfloor heating was flanked by two plunge-baths, hot and cold. On the far side of the fire, originally concealed from view, are the baths for women.

Beyond the baths is the convent of Santa Catalina, dating from 1520 but incorporating the tower of an older Moorish building, with wooden balconies and shutters, and at no. 43 is the Casa de Castril (1539), with a plateresque doorway and a massive stone stair inside leading into a delightful patio. Opposite is another church, San Pedro y Pablo, containing good ceilings. From here, if you have the legs and lungs, you can strike up the Calle de Zafra to the left. Your reward is a beguiling ramble along cobbled alleys and up flights of steps, through tiny squares and past cypresses that wave their finger-tips over the walls of secret gardens. Hidden among them is the mouldering façade of San Juan, the first Christian church in Granada, and at the top is San Nicolas. This church has been restored since a fire in 1932, but the view from it is worth every huff and puff of the climb. Before you the Alhambra's russet towers and walls rise above the trees of the Darro ravine: and beyond them are the snows of the highest mountains south of the Alps.

A couple of hundred metres behind the church is the Puerta Nueva, a fortified gateway set in a fine stretch of thirteenth-century walls. West from here, along the top of the hill, is the oldest part of Moorish Granada, once the site of the forum and basilica of Roman Iliberis. Near the western end of it are two interesting post-Roman relics, one Christian, the other Moorish. The convent of Santa Isabel is *in clausura*, but

---

Good legs and lungs are needed for a stroll through the Albaicin, the oldest inhabited sector of Granada and the original seat of government.

Plateresque detailing by Sebastian de Alcantara on the
renaissance church of Santa Ana, Granada.

a caretaker in the house that faces you inside the courtyard will show you the church, with an excellent *artesonado* ceiling, and elaborate *trompe l'oeil* frescoes filling the east end. Further west, down a side-alley past the church of San Miguel, is one of Granada's few surviving Moorish palaces, the Daralhorra, built on the site of the castle that preceded the Alhambra. Once the home of Boabdil's mother – Ayesha la Horra, 'the Chaste' – it retains some of its interior decoration, and a patio which, though simpler and more domestic, recalls the Alhambra.

There are other distinguished buildings hidden away down in the new city. About a kilometre north of the cathedral is the hospital of San Juan de Dios, with an indifferent church but two splendid patios. Round the corner is the grandest of the city's monasteries, San Jeronimo. The sixteenth-century church is the tomb of Gonzalo de Cordoba, the Gran Capitan whose title has named so many Spanish streets. The country's most famous warrior after El Cid, he fought in the Reconquest, and later against the Turks and French in Greece and Italy. The monastery's chief glory is its cloister, double-storeyed, almost romanesque in style, with seven wonderful doorways by Siloé.

North of here are the Hospital Real and the Cartuja, one notable for its exterior, the other for its interior. The former is renaissance and plateresque, the latter is so exuberantly rococo that it makes the churches of Priego (*see* p. 141) look positively diffident. It is a supreme example of its style and period, but its effect, in Lowe's words, suggests the combined efforts of extravagant baroque builders and a gang of crazed pastrycooks.

At the far end of the Albaicin, on the slopes of Sacromonte, are the caves where gypsies stage displays of flamenco dancing. The performance may not be true flamenco nor the dancers gypsies, but the spectacle is unique. There is much debate as to its origin. The word flamenco may be derived from Flemish or flamingo, both of which seem equally implausible. Far from being Flemish, the music is thought to have oriental antecedents, both Arabic and Jewish, and to have been adopted and modified by the gypsies. At the heart of flamenco is the *cante jondo*, the deep song: eerie and

magical, with its wailing and cascading quarter-notes, it sounds – and traditionally is – the product of extreme emotion, whether religious or amatorial. The gypsies have embellished the performance and enhanced its commercial value with much stamping and frothing of frilled skirts, and by the use of castanets, but the truer accompaniment, as can be heard at any fair in Andalusia, is the clapping of hands.

The best view of Granada is from the N342 to Murcia and Almeria. The road passes above the city and offers a wider panorama than that from San Nicolas – as though you have pulled back on a zoom lens – since the Albaicin itself is now in the foreground, contributing an additional stretch of red walls and towers. The road climbs through pine-woods, and the Sierra Nevada unfolds on the right. After a few kilometres, aficionados of Federico García Lorca, poet, dramatist and exponent of the *cante jondo*, should turn left up a small road to Viznar. This little village has an eighteenth-century archbishop's palace, above which a road runs up the mountainside along a watercourse, passing a slope on the right where hundreds of Republican bodies were buried during the Civil War. A little further, near a spring which once supplied the whole Albaicin (Ford said it bubbled up in a column several metres high), is a plaque marking the spot where Lorca is believed to have been shot on 19 August 1936. The spring, now called the Fuente Grande, was known to the Moors as the Spring of Tears.

Back on the highway, the road climbs to reach 1390 metres at the Puerto de la Mora, after which the scenery opens out into scrub peppered with pink rocks. There are high blue peaks in the distance, and watercourses where pale yellow poplars shine against the sun. The road surface is good and the traffic scant. Soon the valley becomes a flat plain fringed with wind-eroded dunes and sandstone outcrops. Thirty kilometres beyond the pass is the village of Purullena, where the highway is lined with pottery shops, most of them selling brightly-coloured dishes and jugs that have in fact come from further east. The designs incline to the garish, although the jugs make appropriate dispensers for *sangría*, that deceptively refreshing concoction of red wine, lemonade and chopped fruit

Left The hospital of San Juan de Dios in Granada, the first to be built by the saint's Order of Hospitallers.

Above A roadside pottery stall at Purullena. The motifs of birds, roses and pomegranates are traditional, but colours and glazes have coarsened over the years.

The cathedral at Guadix was built on Moorish foundations, which may account for its unusual orientation: the main façade faces south.

served in the beach restaurants . . . laced, if they know their job, with a slug of brandy. Granada has its own traditional ceramic designs, with pomegranates (the city's heraldic device) and birds in subaqueous shades of blue and green: but such ware has become scarce, and you will not find·it here.

Five minutes later, the old centre of Guadix rises dramatically beside the road, a tall row of golden palaces dominated by the cathedral. Inside the walls is a delightful assortment of ancient buildings, all within close walking distance of one another. Dominating a little square is the south face of the cathedral, designed by Siloé in 1549. It is a stirring extravaganza of gold stone, with four doors separated by jutting clusters of pillars, a good population of statues, and a row of stone cannon bluffing a threat from the top. The interior, a scaled-down version of Granada cathedral, is disappointing by comparison, apart from the finely carved choir-stalls. Guadix claims to have established the first Christian bishopric in Spain, and this cathedral was built over a mosque which itself was superimposed on

a Visigothic church. Before that the town was the Roman colony of Acci. Earlier still it was a Carthaginian settlement, the home of Hannibal's wife Himilce.

Opposite the cathedral is the entrance to the Plaza Mayor, or Plaza de la Paloma, a well-proportioned arcaded square which retains its renaissance charm despite the battering it received in the Civil War. Another alley, signposted to the *alcazaba*, leads to the upper part of the town. The houses along the way have elegant seventeenth-century façades, one with a loggia on top, another idiosyncratically colour-washed in pink, the only pink building you are likely to see in Andalusia. On the right is a convent, and ahead and a little below the road is another finer one, that of Santiago the Moor-slayer. The space in front of its church gives scope to admire one of the finest of all plateresque doorways, and there is a handsome *artesonado* ceiling inside.

The castle is very early – ninth-century – and unassuming. The entrance is through a seminary, and the bailey is a scruffy playground, with a trio of small sandy towers reminiscent of *Beau Geste*. But the view is worth the climb. The valley is rimmed with fretted cliffs, behind which, to the south, is the ever-present Sierra Nevada. In this direction the tufa ravines are close, and you can see that they are riddled with caves. This is the most distinctive sector of Guadix, the suburb of the troglodytes.

There are various approaches, of which the easiest is to turn off the main road on the Granada side of the town centre. You soon find yourself driving through a strange lumpy landscape, like a badly stuffed mattress, from which jut crags and cones of compacted clay. Many of the cliffs are sliced away to create mini-façades, whitewashed and pierced with doors and windows.

More disconcerting are the chimneys, which sprout like young asparagus from the hillsides, often far from any visible dwelling. Inside, the rooms are squarely cut and whitewashed and like any Andalusian village house until you become aware of the lack of windows. The inhabitants will tell you that the interior temperature is exceptionally equable, cool in summer and warm in winter. Most houses have electric light and television (plumbing is another matter) and in Puru-llena, which also has its troglodyte district, there is an underground night-club, and the upwardly mobile park their cars in underground garages. More than a third of Guadix's population live in caves, one of which has eleven rooms. This mole-like mentality means house-building is cheap: the material is free, and a practiced worker can cut a room of 15 square metres in four days.

Fifteen kilometres beyond Guadix, in another flat plain, you can see to the right an improbably regular little hillock like an anthill on which is set, in a manner so random that it seems to be slipping off to one side, a little toy castle. This is La Calahorra, and in one sense it is a toy: inside the military shell, with its pepper-pot corner towers, is the earliest renaissance architecture in Spain: an exquisite early sixteenth-century patio in the Italian style, on two storeys, with slender pillars and dainty carvings, and handsome salons giving off it. But it is only open one day a week, and the final climb to it is steep. The road to the little village continues south over the Sierra Nevada, via a high and forbiddingly deserted pass. If you are considering this route, enquire first whether the road is open.

Only scant ruins remain of the castle at Fiñana, a couple of dozen kilometres further down the main Murcia road, but the prettiness of the village around it´ warrants the little loop off the highway. Beyond it the broad valley dries out to a total barrenness, where nothing grows in the stony soil except clumps of yellow genista. Then come the first clues that the Mediterranean lies ahead – almonds, eucalyptus thickets and vines. But they soon vanish as the terrain grows ever bleaker. After passing the grander but less accessible castle of Gergal, the road heads for the great massif of the Sierra de Alhamilla through a rocky desert of bleached and eroded cliffs and ridges, livid and distorted and glinting with quartz. This landscape is different from anything else in Andalusia, but familiar to anyone who has watched cowboy films. Indeed, at one point a glance to the right gives a glimpse of what appears to be a Nevada ghost town, with a ruined church and the shells of adobe houses.

But this is not a hallucination. Turn left at the next main intersection, 18 kilometres past Gergal, on to the N340 to Murcia. Ahead, the keep of Tabernas rears dramatically above the road, the best of the three castles since La Calahorra, but before reaching it turn right down a dusty track signposted to the *decorados*, or film-sets. The track doubles back under the road and bumps along a dry river-bed lined with tamarisks. And suddenly, on a rise, is a ghost town, or rather two, a silver-mining town and a Mexican village. This is Mini Hollywood. Over a hundred Westerns have been filmed here, but when I visited it in May the place was so eerily deserted that I kept peering uneasily over my shoulder for the arrival of the horsemen in the black hats. The dusty streets outside the false-fronted stores, bar and hotel were littered with the appropriate props – carts, a gallows and motley interior fitments such as a piano and a brass-fitted bar-front. I would not want to be there in high summer: apart from the crowds – gun-fights are staged for the tourists – the heat must be intense.

South towards the coast, the jumbled badlands gradually give way to a featureless wasteland, and soon you are amid Almeria's sprawling suburbs. The city is now largely modern, but its history is extensive. When the Caliphate of Cordoba broke up in the early eleventh century, Almeria was one of the thirty-odd city-states that declared their independence, and for half a century it became the most important capital in Moorish Spain. Its silks were famous throughout Europe, and its corsairs were as feared as those of the Barbary Coast. Previously it had been a neolithic settlement, a Carthaginian harbour, and the Portus Magnus of the Romans, their main outlet for trade with Italy and the East.

It was to Almeria that Boabdil fled when he was thrown out of Granada by his father, Muley Hassan, thereby ceasing for a while to be the Boy King. He had in the meantime acquired another nickname after his capture by the Christians at Lucena: *El Zogoybi*, the Unlucky One. Unlucky or not, he was still a threat to the rulers in Granada, and was pursued to Almeria by his uncle El Zagal, the greatest of the Moorish warriors, who took over the kingdom of Granada on the death of

201

Left The castle of La Calahorra, built by Italian craftsmen for the bastard son of a cardinal.

Above The Mini-Hollywood sets are still occasionally used to make films and television commercials, but nowadays the main income is from tourists.

Maritime motifs in Almeria, once the 'Great Harbour' of the Romans.

Muley Hassan. But Boabdil escaped and fled to the Christians. This was the second time he had evaded his rivals, as his redoubtable mother Ayesha is said to have let him down in a basket from a window in the Comares tower in the Alhambra. Alternately escaping and falling captive, fighting and fleeing, the hapless Boabdil was a prime cause and perpetuator of the inner war that did more to destroy the kingdom of Granada than all the exploits of the Christian armies.

His scourge El Zagal later returned to this region under very different circumstances. In 1489, after the loss of the key city of Baza, east of Granada, he surrendered Almeria to the Christians, together with Guadix, Tabernas, and other Moorish fortresses. In return he was given money, some salt mines in the Alpujarras (the district to which Boabdil too was soon to be exiled) and 2000 subjects. This was a poor substitute for his previous power and the glories of the Alhambra, and in disgust he left Spain and went to Morocco, where the Moorish invasion had originated. Here, despite his record, he was imprisoned, blinded, and turned out to end his days wandering as a beggar.

Almeria is not my favourite town, but its old kernel retains some charm. The cathedral, designed by Siloé after an earthquake in 1522 wrecked the former mosque, has a truculently military air, supposedly because it served as a refuge against the Barbary pirates. From here you can stroll to the Plaza Vieja, whose arcaded façades breathe a shuttered drowsiness, anomalous in so bustling a city, and on past the eighteenth-century convent of Santa Clara to the *alcazaba*. But even the locals will dissuade you from wandering alone through this sector at night: 'there are many poor people there' is the euphemism for the rise in street-crime.

The *alcazaba* is immense, and so immaculately restored that it is a gift to the film-makers from Mini-Hollywood. It was originally begun in the tenth century by Abderrahman III (the caliph who completed the mosque at Cordoba), but was ruined in the 1522 earthquake. The curtain walls continue up the slope of a neighbouring hill, where there was once another castle, and enclose a narrow Eden of shrubs, flowers and streams. From the battlements, re-equipped with their early Moorish merlons, there is a fine and contrasting view, dun and dusty to the north and west, deep Mediterranean blue to the south.

The water-front has the wanderlust excitement of any port, with big ships moored at the quay: but for beaches you must head east or west. The landscape to the east is a dejected hangover from the desert of the hinterland, but the shore is dramatically rocky in places, with small cliff-ringed beaches offering good snorkelling, and fishing settlements now developed for tourism. The resources of this coast begin on the near side of the Cabo de Gata, the eastern arm of Almeria's bay and now a national park, where there

Oranges are among the many crops grown in the intensive farming belt around Almeria, although Spain's main orange plantations are further east.

are salt-pans and crystal caves. They effectively terminate nearly a hundred kilometres away at Mojacar, whose Arab hill-houses are now filled with boutiques and blonde northern Europeans.

To the west another new industry has ruined the coastline even more effectively than tourism: intensive farming. The entire coastal plain is gift-wrapped in plastic sheeting, beneath which the local farmers, once amongst the poorest in Spain, now make fortunes by raising three crops a year. The result is a flood of out-of-season vegetables, fruit and flowers for the European community, but this has been achieved at some cost to both the ecology and the local social system: there are warnings about the effect of the constant irrigation on the water-table, and the sudden wealth has reputedly caused a sharp rise in suicides and alcoholism.

Marooned between the plastic and the sea are some dismal resorts, of which the best are beyond Roquetas de Mar. At least the beaches are good, and unlike the western Costa del Sol the building is low-rise: but if you are touring this region my advice would be to head inland. Behind the coastal highway are two attractive hill-villages, Felix and Enix, 1000 metres up in the Sierra de Gador above Aguadulce. This is too high for intensive farming, and agriculture is still of the old, back-breaking kind that depends on the mule and the single-bladed plough – an instrument little changed from that depicted on the pottery of the ancient Greeks. The whitewashed contortions of the village streets are delightful and the views extensive, but although the steepness of the approach roads affords some protection against tourism, these places are too close to the shore to remain immune. To find a community still untouched by change, you must visit the other side of the coastal mountains, and seek out one of the most secret and dramatic landscapes in all Andalusia: the region known as the Alpujarras, the inland valleys that run parallel to the coast from Motril, south of Granada, almost to the border with Murcia.

This was the heartland of the Moors. While the other towns and fortresses around Granada crumbled before the Christian cannon, the Alpujarras continued to send men and supplies. At the end of the campaign, it was to this region that El Zagal and Boabdil were both exiled, although their pathetic kingdom was in a remoter part of it, north of Tabernas. Once the Christians were in full control, they soon reneged on the conditions signed at Santa Fe, and Isabella allowed her devotion to get the better of her humanity, as she had with the foundation of the Inquisition. Although the Muslims had been promised freedom of religion, customs, laws, dress and private property, they were now abruptly offered the alternatives of Christian baptism or exile. Further punitive decrees continued during the sixteenth century, leading to a full-scale rebellion in the Alpujarras in 1568, with appalling atrocities on both sides; after which King Philip II decided to uproot the majority of the Muslims from Andalusia and transplant them in the north.

This was not the last diaspora. In the early seventeenth century all Muslims were evicted from Spain. As Isabella had done the same to the Jews in 1492, the Christians had now succeeded in eliminating the two most talented and energetic sub-sections of their population. Thereafter, as the history books show, Spain's fortunes declined.

For centuries the Alpujarras have been mined for marble, salt, silver, lead and gold: and it was one of the centres of the silk trade, which brought great wealth to the region. 'When Almeria was Almeria', runs an ancient ditty, 'Granada was merely its farm.' A couple of centuries ago the looms finally fell silent, superseded by the newer technology and materials of northern Europe, but not before the industry had bequeathed a number of words to the English language: scarlet was derived from *iskalaton*, our tabby cat owes it name to *attabi*, a striped taffeta from Baghdad, and buckram was an adaptation of Bokhara.

Today the Alpujarras have no monuments to their history, but are rich in grapes, water, wine, ham and scenery. In the twenties they attracted another refugee, the author Gerald Brenan, who rented a house in

Rich in minerals, poor in vegetation: the badlands north of Almeria.

the remote village of Yegen for a number of years between 1920–34. His book *South from Granada* describes his life there and the visits of his literary friends, mostly members of the Bloomsbury Group. Lytton Strachey could not stand the solitude, and warned Virginia Woolf against it: 'It's death. Death!'

To reach the Alpujarras from Almeria, head north back towards Granada, but turn off left after 12 kilometres onto the road that follows the Andarax valley. Here, where the badlands of the cowboy country meet the riverside vineyards, the colour contrasts are intoxicating, the pink and yellow and white of the wrinkled sand-banks commingling with the piercing green of the vines. These grapes are for eating, not wine, and are grown on head-high pergolas, from which the fat bunches hang into the dappled shade beneath. After the bare wilderness of the drive down from Granada, it becomes apparent that this extraordinary land of Andalusia has put on yet another face. This too changes again as the road climbs to leave the river, into the high land to the south, planted with olives.

The little hamlet of Fondon is the first to offer a roadside bar. Its interior décor is of a searing nastiness, but the *tapas* are substantial enough to make an adequate meal: three kinds of sausage, meatballs, bacon and two kinds of pork, as well as the fish which is staple fare down on the coast. The wine is a disconcerting pinky-orange and tastes like unfortified sherry. A better local wine is the rosé of the Contraviesa massif away to the south-west, sold throughout the region as *vino de la costa*.

Ahead is a wide green valley, behind which the Sierra Nevada has reappeared. It can be crossed here by the road which leads north from the next village and over the top to La Calahorra: but our way lies west, across a ridge which marks the watershed between the Andarax and the next river. An immense vista opens up to the south, and the terrain is fissured with vast runnels in the multi-coloured earth. Brenan used the long earth-bridges between them to walk from village to village, and explains that this great valley was once a lake: when it drained away it left a deep bed of argillaceous sand, which centuries of rain and wind

have sculpted to its present shape.

Stay on the C332 and in a few kilometres you reach Brenan's village, Yegen. The road to it passes through Valor – where a fiesta in mid September re-enacts the battles between Moors and Christians during the 1568 rebellion – then climbs steeply through olives and lush greenery filled with birdsong and the sound of rushing water. Yegen looks out across the wide valley to the bulk of the Sierra de la Contraviesa that shuts off the sea. As far as the eye can see, the red earth has been weeded bare, presumably by hand or by mule-plough, since there is no room for a tractor between the trees. The air is fresh and windy. The village is smaller than Brenan describes it, and very quiet. Brenan's house is identifiable by a plaque on its wall, but since his time it has been divided into three. All that can be seen is the patio, and the loggia he describes on the top floor, a common local construction used for drying corn-cobs and red peppers and tomatoes.

Looking down on Yegen from the main road you realize that the villages in the Alpujarras are built in a style found nowhere else, flat-roofed like Berber villages in north Africa. They are not as pretty as the otherwise universal tiled equivalent, but there is no denying the drama of Yegen's situation. 'I had not been there a day' says Brenan after a five-year absence 'before the old impression of height and stillness, of fields of air stretching before me, and channels of water running behind came over me again. . . . Standing then on the flat roof one saw the earth falling away sheer on every side, as though one stood on the prow of a ship that was sailing off across a petrified ocean.'

Even so, Brenan's part of the Alpujarras is not the prettiest: it can be trumped if you continue down the GR421 to the western end. One route is via a right-hand loop that snakes up into the mountains to reach Trevelez, the highest village in Spain, famous for the Serrano hams which are sent here to be cured in its frosty caves. According to Brenan, the climate is not

Beires, in the Alpujarras, landlocked between the Sierra Nevada and the coastal mountain range.

the only reason for the excellence of the end-product: sorcery in these parts is more common at high altitudes, he says, and the hams are muttered over by witches.

A more direct route west is along the narrowing valley of the Guadalfeo. At the junction with the C333 turn right to Orgiva and then immediately right again. The road climbs steeply, bypassing two or three villages, through mountains which are softer than the Serrania de Ronda, lacking dramatic peaks or cliffs, but magnificently folded on themselves, and lapped in foliage that filters the light and modulates the distant colours to blue and purple. Below the road the land falls away steeply to a river far below. Round a corner at the head of a narrow valley appear the snows of Mulhacen, the highest mountain in Spain, named after Boabdil's father Muley Hassan, and below it are the last two villages, white and flat-roofed, clinging to the hillside like martins' nests. Set at a height of 1400 metres, Bubion and Capileira could hardly be more remote: yet on entering them it is immediately apparent that they are very different from Yegen. This is a resort area, and the narrow streets are full of bars, restaurants, souvenir shops and hostels.

For a few weeks a year the road above Capileira is open through to the ski resort of Solynieve on the far side of the mountains, and so on to Granada. But do not venture this way without first checking that it is clear. Alternatively, retrace the road to the valley bottom and turn right to Lanjaron. This is a spa town with an old-fashioned courtliness which is all its own. Turn-of-the-century hotels and stately houses with flower-decked balconies line the shady main street, and you would think yourself in northern Europe were it not for the sun and the eucalyptus trees. Visitors still flock to the baths, seeking relief from ailments that vary from sinusitis to nervous tension, and the town's name is a familiar sight on the labels of its bottled mineral water, drawn from 42 springs at the rate of 400,000 litres a day. Lanjaron has an old sector below the main road, and lower still a miniature castle sits on a pimple of rock and surveys the valley.

Six kilometres beyond Lanjaron you hit the main road between Granada and the coast. Those who

hanker for the sea, or are flying home from Malaga, can turn left down the N323 to Motril, through a dramatic gorge, or branch off onto the new highway which reaches the coast near Salobreña. This town and its neighbour to the west, Almuñecar, are of great antiquity, with castle-topped piles of white houses rising like islands from the plantations of sugar and loquats, custard-apples and avocadoes. The *plasticultura* is less prevalent here, and both towns are worth a visit.

Salobreña is the smaller and the more intact. Its castle was deemed so impregnable by the Moorish kings that they used it for the safe-keeping of their treasure and of any relatives who might be a threat to the throne. 'The palace was adorned with fountains', says Irving, 'and delicious gardens and perfumed baths; a harem of beauties was at the command of the royal captives, and music and the dance beguiled the lagging hours. Nothing was denied them but the liberty to depart.' The castle can be reached by car, with some difficulty, up steep streets cobbled in black and white. It has been thoroughly restored, and is beautifully planted with mimosa, aloes and canna lilies between the concentric circles of its walls: from the top there are magnificent views up and down the coast, and inland to the Sierra Nevada. The church, near the bottom of the town, has a jumble of roofs and a Moorish south doorway in purple and green. When I last visited it, the statues for the Easter parades were being prepared on their floats, and the air inside was heavy with the smells of varnish and paint.

Almuñecar is larger and older: to the delight of English-speaking visitors its Phoenician name was Sexi. The Moorish town centre is almost invisible behind modern tower-blocks, and can only be visited on foot: but once penetrated, it is a delight. The alleyways are paved with tiles or cobbled in black-and-white patterns – whorls and chequers, curlicues and herring-bone. They lead past leafy squares, beneath arches and up flights of steps, until at last they

---

Capileira: the road that crosses the Sierra Nevada north from here is the highest in Europe.

reach the castle at the top. This is more ramshackle than that of Salobreña, and a tower beside the entrance is slumped sideways as though exhausted by its history. Inside is a dramatic but somewhat spine-chilling cemetery, where the tiered sarcophagi, of whitewashed masonry, are ranged along the cypress-lined paths like the ruins of a haunted town.

West of here is the only unspoilt part of the Costa del Sol. Nature has left no room for tower-blocks or intensive farming, and the round-shouldered mountains roll down to the sea, crowned with clifftop watch-towers. Here and there the old Arab terraces, once filled with mulberries for the silk trade, are now being dusted-off and planted with avocadoes: and inland little white farmhouses are surrounded with rectangular enclosures on the hillsides where the grapes are spread in the sunshine, to be converted into raisins. Beyond the agreeable resort of Nerja, where there are spectacular caves, the road continues through deteriorating scenery to Malaga and the horrors of the Marbella gold-coast.

For those returning directly to Granada from Lanjaron, there is one more sight to see. Or rather a setting: the stage rather than the play itself, which took place half a millennium ago. A few kilometres north along the N323, the terrain soon widens into the Happy Valley of the Muslims, the basin that held their upland farms. It looks less happy now – the view behind you is´

Salobreña, whose castle was used by the Moorish kings for locking away their treasure and unwanted relatives.

better – but the Sierra Nevada has reappeared on your right to accompany you into Granada. After 25 kilometres, past the town of Padul, a cluster of bars and hotels marks the pass named the Ultimo Suspiro del Moro, the Moor's Last Sigh.

On 2 January 1492, Boabdil passed out of the Alhambra through the Tower of the Seven Storeys, crossed the River Genil, and handed over the keys of Granada to Ferdinand of Aragon at the Hermitage of San Sebastian. This still survives, a kilometre south of the Plaza del Humilladero where the Catholic monarchs sank to their knees on seeing the Cross displayed from the topmost tower of the Alhambra. While the cannon roared and the bells sounded, Boabdil and his retinue departed south until they reached the pass. There, like Lot, he turned round, for his last glimpse of the city. He would have needed sharp eyes at this distance, but tradition relates that he wept to see what he was leaving behind. For this weakness he was berated by his mother: 'You do well to weep like a woman for what you failed to defend like a man.'

This is not quite the last that history relates of Boabdil. Like his uncle before him, he could not stand his lonely exile in the Alpujarras for long, and four years later he crossed to Fez in Morocco, where, according to Trevelyan, there are still families who keep keys to houses in Granada. Here, surprisingly, he fared better than El Zagal. He is said to have lived until 1536, when he was killed in battle at the age of 63, beside a river which carried his body out to sea. In the words of one chronicler, the Unlucky One thus exemplified by his death 'the scornful caprice of fortune; dying in defence of the kingdom of another, after wanting spirit to die in defence of his own'.

Index